News Literacy, Informed Citizens and Consumer-Driven Media: The

Future Landscape of American Journalism

A thesis
submitted to the faculty of
the College of Arts and Sciences of
Georgetown University
in partial fulfillment of
the degree of
Bachelor of Arts
in American Studies

Caroline Elizabeth Klibanoff

Washington, D.C.
April 20, 2012

Copyright 2012 Lulu
by Caroline Elizabeth Klibanoff
All Rights Reserved

ISBN 978-1-105-72589-0

News Literacy, Informed Citizens and Consumer-Driven Media: The Future Landscape of American Journalism

Caroline Elizabeth Klibanoff
Under the Supervision of Dr. Kimberly Meltzer
Georgetown University

Abstract

Today, Americans face the challenge of information overload through increasingly accessible mediums, making it harder to identify valuable information and to move fluently and efficiently through social media, news and entertainment platforms. And yet, because of this profound connectivity, user engagement levels are at an all-time high. Individual consumers have more power than ever to shape the changing digital world and demand high-quality information merely by connecting with news sources online. The American press, which once suffered as a result of this technological revolution, now faces increased opportunities to make news accessible and creative, and has the chance to serve a new generation of proactive Web consumers.

It is of utmost importance, then, that this very consumer class is as informed and educated as possible in regards to the value of accurate, verified journalism and high-quality reporting, in order to demand a better journalistic product and to fulfill the American ideal of an informed, engaged citizenry. In recent years, news literacy education programs have begun to tackle this through secondary schooling, implementing tenets of news and media literacy into public school curriculum in civics, history, government and English. Currently these programs are small-scale and spread through a grassroots approach, so it is pertinent to study them now to determine a future course of action. In this thesis I perform a case study of news literacy programs in secondary schools and place my findings into the context of the modern media landscape in order to determine if news literacy education can help create more critical consumers of media, and what role a more news-literate public might play in driving demand for a better, thriving and tech-savvy journalistic product.

While news literacy levels clearly must be raised among youth for the sake of civic responsibility, and the existing educational programs make good progress towards this, ultimately I find that implementation through the education system proves insufficient unless made a comprehensive part of middle- and high-school curriculum, embedded as deeply as civics and critical reading. One alternative is to teach news literacy in fields that are more relevant and effective, outside the education system: social media, mobile and tablet applications, and extracurricular or recreational programs. The combined force of the technology industry, journalists and educators is essential to raising the news literacy rate, and advocates for news literacy must insist on the collaborative involvement of technology, digital media and the Internet in developing and teaching news literacy principles.

Acknowledgements

The completion of this thesis would not have been possible without the assistance of various individuals and parties. I would first like to thank the American Studies department at Georgetown University for a wonderful four years in exploration of our nation, and to the many professors in History, English, Music, Theology and Sociology who helped round out my understanding of American culture so that I might approach this thesis with a more nuanced sense of history.

Many thanks to my advisor, Dr. Kim Meltzer, who has seen this project take many iterations from the beginning and who offered constant support; to Colva Weissenstein, Lily Hughes and Garrison LeMasters for guidance throughout the senior thesis seminar; and to my teaching advisor Andy Lewandowski in offering helpful critique and suggestions. I am grateful to Diana Owen, department head and IRB expert, and Bernie Cook, director of Film & Media Studies, who have been especially helpful in navigating this process; to Hugh Cloke and Elizabeth McKeown for the solid foundation in AmCiv I and II; and of course, to my classmates in American Studies who have made the last four years so much fun.

My research could not have been completed without the generosity and assistance of various news literacy experts, including Alan Miller, Maureen Freeman and Whitney Allgood of the News Literacy Project; Sissel McCarthy of Emory University; Elia Powers; Dean Miller and Howard Schneider of the Center for News Literacy; Eliza Ford of E.L. Haynes Charter School; the English classes at

Bethesda – Chevy Chase High School; and the wisdom of many journalists and colleagues, including Andy Alexander, Ken Paulson, and Charles Overby.

Finally, I am forever indebted to my wonderful parents Hank and Laurie for their love, attention and tolerance of frequent one-sided phone calls, to my sisters for the solidarity in support of the journalism we grew up with, and to my brilliant and loyal friends who not only listened to me talk about Knight reports and the power of the Internet for nine months, but jumped on the bandwagon with great enthusiasm and on occasion preached the news literacy gospel themselves.

Table of Contents

Ch. 1: Introduction..1

Ch. 2: Review of Literature..8

    Understanding the 'Future of Media' Conversation........................8

    Production-Side Approaches...10

    Consumers Choose the News..14

    Information Needs of a Changing Audience....................................16

    Media Literacy: A Savvier Pro-Sumer..21

    News Literacy Education...24

Ch. 3: Research Method..33

Ch. 4: An Overview of News Literacy Programs...40

    Origins of the News Literacy Movement...40

    The News Literacy Project..42

    The Center for News Literacy at Stony Brook..................................48

    News Literacy Initiatives Outside the Classroom............................53

Ch. 5: Case Study Findings..59

    Bethesda – Chevy Chase High School and NLP..............................59

    Case Study 1: Honors English..60

    Case Study 2: Journalism 2...65

Ch. 6: Conclusions...73

    Immediate conclusions...73

    Suggestions for Improvement of Existing Models...........................76

    Proposals for Moving Beyond the Classroom..................................79

    Disruption and Opportunity: America at a Crossroads....................84

Bibliography..87

Chapter 1: An Introduction

In the spring of 2008, I graduated from high school and my father stepped down from his role as managing editor of *The Atlanta Journal Constitution* after a lifetime spent in newspaper reporting and editing. I had followed and internalized the rise and fall of newspapers since childhood. In the prosperous days of the 1990s, my dad worked at one of the most thriving, exciting newspapers in America, *The Philadelphia Inquirer*, and things were good for my family. My sisters and I bummed around the newsroom on days off from school and Take Your Daughter to Work Day, amusing ourselves with red editing pencils and gazing dumbfounded at the massive machinery in the printing and circulation hangar. We had three newspapers delivered to our home every morning, most of my parents' friends were journalists, and I gained personal insight into the power of the "Fourth Estate" and its key role in shaping American democracy.[1]

It wasn't until the decade progressed and the Internet grew massively in scope that the *Inquirer*, like other large newspapers, began to see circulation drop and advertisement revenue decline. From 1999 to 2003, more or less my middle school years, I was privy to tense conversations about "buyouts" and "restructuring" and "cutting costs," ultimately resulting in my father's departure from *The Inquirer* and his move to *The Atlanta Journal-Constitution*. In Atlanta, those talks continued, varying in tone from hopeful to foreboding as the top editors, my father

---

[1] The news media in America is colloquially referred to as the "Fourth Estate," an authoritative but unofficial institution existing outside the three branches of government.

included, discussed different payment models and newsroom organization structures. None of it can truly be said to have worked: the digital age prevailed over print circulation, as it does today; no one could figure out a genuinely profitable business model for a digital product; and perhaps most significantly, a cultural shift took place among my generation as we learned to expect easy and free access to media of all forms, news and entertainment alike. It wasn't just a "perfect storm" for the traditional, established press – it was a storm that caught news leadership off guard, one that pitted the tech industry against the news industry in a detrimental few years.

By the time I graduated from high school in 2008, being firmly of my generation, I began to adopt some of the enthusiasm for the sheer possibilities of the Internet that would prove only to increase in college. I was an early adopter to new technologies and saw social media, music sharing, and blogging go through a number of iterations even before the rise of Web 2.0. And yet, knowing the long hours my dad worked for the newspaper, and his deep care for every headline, photo and sentence that went into the finished product, plus my own work experience in newspaper journalism and blogging, I found myself caught between two worlds. The press and the Web should have entered the 21st century together, armed with the power to transform the American news media into something great. Instead, the two existed at odds while profit margins drained low and the American public grew increasingly distrustful and uninformed about the press itself.

Four years later, the news industry has presumably weathered the worst of the storm. The nostalgic ties to a printed product and to major legacy outlets – CNN, NBC, *The New York Times*, *The Washington Post* – that once hindered progress have been muted in favor of a full-on embrace of technology. News leadership, meaning producers and editors, have mostly gotten on board with using social media, data mining and mobile or tablet platforms in news production and similar tools in marketing. There is a new optimism surrounding the future landscape of journalism where it intersects with technology; the more these two industries collaborate the more innovative the possibilities become. For example, tech giant Mozilla recently launched a partnership with the Knight Foundation to explore fresh solutions to improve journalism, and other start-ups like Storify, Spot.us, ProPublica, and Fuego have manipulated the power of the Web to build new journalistic structures.

Financial problems persist: the public has gained access to the press in its desired forms for free, with the exception of a few successful paywalls. Local papers continue to work under great duress and many have shut down.[2] Though the overall sentiment of most Americans towards traditional news media is one of distrust, that is slowly changing, and the media is one of the few industries experiencing an increase in trust among its users, perhaps due to the connectivity of social media.[3] Social media connects citizens more closely than ever with the press, resulting in a

---

[2] Smith, Erica. PaperCuts, 2012. www.newspaperlayoffs.com. Accessed 3 March 2012. PaperCuts is a valuable database and map system that keeps track of the devastating number of newspaper jobs lost and paper closures across America since 2007.

[3] Edelman, "2012 Trust Barometer Infographic," *Edelman Insights*. 2012. http://www.slideshare.net/EdelmanInsights/trust-bar-fin. Accessed 1 March 2012.

highly engaged consumer class free to comment, respond, re-blog, or tweet at articles, journalists, or institutions, and free to select their sources based on personal preference. This "engagement" has become the focus of much innovation and study as producers realize the significance of consumer choice as it relates to news sources.[4]

Americans have moved from an audience of passive spectators, as with television broadcasts or a daily print newspaper delivered at one's doorstep, to interactive participants, digesting and outputting news and information at rapid speeds. This behavior originates in social settings ("social media") but parlays into news digestion with significant consequences, blurring the lines between "news" and "information," between recreational consumption (i.e. watching a YouTube video) and work (i.e. citing a YouTube video) and between citizen-recorded data and professional journalism. The current media landscape directly challenges the necessity of traditional or legacy news outlets and the value of professional, verified and objective journalism, and simultaneously empowers the individual consumer to wield his or her influence upon the press.

As a result, it becomes more important than ever to look closely at the needs, desires and demands of the consumer class (perhaps more aptly referred to as "participants" since their primary act is to engage, not purchase) who drive these

---

[4] Throughout this thesis I will emphasize the engagement of news consumers through the medium of the Internet. I realize that Internet access and ease of use often falls along socioeconomic lines and only 88% of Americans have access to the Web. However, this is more than double the amount with access ten years ago, showing a distinct rise in prevalence, and more significantly social media use continues to eclipse almost all other purposes of the Internet, according to Nielsen's U.S. Digital Consumer Report 2012. The Internet's increased relevance to the "offline" world make it a pertinent domain unto itself. The impact of the Web is big, growing, and should be considered an essential factor when looking at any aspect of American culture in the 21st century.

changes in production, as well as if, and how, news corporations, producers and institutions are meeting those needs. This is a relatively new focus, one long familiar to profit-seeking businesses and advertisers, but fresh to news organizations. As media and tech expert Clay Shirky points out, "There has never been a mass market for good journalism in this country. What there used to be was a mass market for print ads, coupled with a mass market for a physical bundle of entertainment, opinion and information."[5] The same can be said for television news interspersed with commercial breaks and entertainment. The old bundle system meant that readers were freed of the responsibility to seek out better news, and certainly freed of the burden of evaluating available news for veracity. There was no real need for news literacy.

And what exactly is news literacy? The News Literacy Project in Bethesda, Md., defines news literacy as "how to know what to believe." News literate people possess the skills to distinguish between verified news, opinion, and spin; to understand the media cycle and landscape; to locate, select and demand trustworthy information; and to use their own voice in a responsible and powerful way to engage with their communities. This is a very modern, of-the-times vision that incorporates the consumer as a powerful, autonomous participant rather than passive audience member, and accounts for the fact that news resides in a number of spheres today, not just the major cable channels and newspapers.

---

[5] Shirky, Clay. "Are Newspapers Finally Figuring Out How to Reward Their Best Customers?" *Paid Content*, Jan. 4 2012 http://paidcontent.org/article/419-are-newspapers-finally-figuring-out-how-to-reward-their-best-customers/P1/ Accessed Jan. 4 2012.

Today, news comes in myriad forms (long, short, micro) and modes (television, newspaper, radio, blogs, web publications, tablet applications, podcasts, mobile devices, and social media). Speed is essential and the 24-hour news cycle is institutionalized. The ease of producing stories and headlines – or simply re-posting them as part of the viral news cycle – means today's news media encompass a dizzying amount of ever-expanding content.[6] Modern consumers have access to an incredible amount of information and yet few resources for sorting and comprehending such data. In such an information deluge, media literacy education and, more specifically, news literacy education, equips citizens with the critical reading tools necessary to locate and evaluate information. It places the onus of responsibility on the public, rather than the press, the Internet, or the government, something that should be seen as an opportunity for citizen empowerment, not an added burden of the digital age. News literacy education is pro-consumer.

It is a pro-news stance as well, supported by the idea that more informed consumers will demand higher-quality news in the forms most convenient and accessible to them priced at market value. News, then, will be improved overall and the monetary value of such news will be determined clearly for producers, who will no longer have to guess at consumers' motivations for pirating or paying for news. As Clay Shirky notes, the current minority of citizens willing to pay for traditional news "are almost by definition people who regard the paper not just as an

---

[6] In this paper I use language that reveals a bias towards newspapers as the primary form of news over television or radio, i.e. "headlines" or "articles." I do not wish to suggest any sort of hierarchy or act with intent, but it is an attempt to use the language of online news since that is the focus of my research. Online news, as it happens, usually follows the format of newspaper journalism (the written word, photographs and art, headlines and bylines) over television or radio, though job titles follow broadcasting tradition: "producer," "manager."

occasional source of interesting articles, but as an essential institution, one whose continued existence is vital."[7]

The task of news literacy education then must be twofold: to teach critical assessment of information sources, of course, but also to cultivate a respect for good journalism (though not necessarily for legacy media sources). Careful and caring consumers signal a far brighter future for American cultural and civic life than indifferent, uninformed ones, and news literacy education is at the heart of this idea. Our task now is to unearth the best possible method for improving news literacy levels among all Americans in the name of civic responsibility.

---

[7] Shirky, "Are Newspapers Finally Figuring Out How to Reward Their Best Customers?"

CHAPTER 2: REVIEW OF LITERATURE

Understanding the 'Future of Media' Conversation

Stepping back from my focus on news literacy to look at the future of journalism at large, the most comprehensive and useful discussion of this subject currently lives in two realms. Official reports sponsored by the U.S. government and media watchdog organizations like the Poynter Institute, the Pew Research Center and the Knight Foundation propose detailed assessments of the current media landscape and plans for reform, while personal blogs and editorials by prominent media scholars and thinkers, often professors of journalism or authors of those very government reports, comment on the cultural consequences of such change. These publications are in conversation with each other and often represent a broad network of journalists, government officials, educators and digital media advocates. Further, as we turn a corner in 2012 technologically, there are increasing instances of journalists partnering with IT groups to discuss the future of journalism, adding a new, productive dimension to past solutions. The narrower news literacy discussion primarily lives where these "hacks and hackers" teams, i.e. collaborations between the press and the tech communities, border with the education reform community, and indeed the triad of education reform, tech innovation and journalism provides fresh hope and opportunity for the field of news literacy.

There have been three major categories for the examination and advancement of American journalism since 2008: production-side news operations, government policy and regulation, and consumer-side reform and demand. The first two have been written about and debated extensively, especially in regards to payment models and how to profit and prosper in the digital age. The third area, looking more closely at the needs and wants of the consumer class, has only recently entered the spotlight. This focus has quickly proven to be worthy of study as it generates innovation and essential questions and touches other realms of current sea change such as education, democracy and government, and the free market of the Internet. To cover the breadth of thought in these three areas, Robert McChesney and Victor Pickard's collection of essays, *Will the Last Reporter Please Turn Out The Lights? The Collapse of Journalism and What Can Be Done to Fix It*, provides a variety of suggestions by media and culture scholars like Eric Alterman, Todd Gitlin, Henry Jenkins, Robert Niles, Renee Hobbs, Clay Shirky, and Michael J. Copps of the Federal Communication Commission. These essays are forward thinking and written by some of the best media minds of our time, but as a collection are inconclusive. For example, as the late C. Edwin Baker, the "leading authority on freedom of the press and the First Amendment," testified before Congress in 2009, "the market alone could not be expected to adequately support the communication needs of a democratic society."[8] His government-intervention strategy bears an entirely different locus of responsibility than that of Renee Hobbs, who places power on the educated consumer, or those of Clay Shirky, who believes

---

[8] McChesney, Robert and Victor Pickard, ed. *Will the Last Reporter Please Turn Out the Lights? The Collapse of Journalism and What Can Be Done to Fix It.* New York: The New Press, 2011. Print, xxi.

most of journalism's ailments result from and can be cured by those in charge of producing it.

Production-Side Approaches

Despite the different directions of these three schools of thought – focusing on news producers, the government, and news consumers – they share a common goal, to reduce the cost and raise the quality of American journalism. Government intervention has been suggested both as a solution for quality control, as evidenced in the seminal FCC report, "The Information Needs of Communities," and as a solution for funding through subsidization of "legacy" outlets like traditional, established papers, radio signals and television stations. Non-journalists lead the way in this realm; David Swensen, Chief Investment Officer at Yale University, proposed that newspapers take on nonprofit status, with endowments from "enlightened philanthropists" to cover costs,[9] while Maryland Senator Ben Cardin introduced the "Newspaper Revitalization Act" bill to make the transition to nonprofit status easier.[10]

The funding question – that is, how to pay for solid journalism— plagues many discussions and prevents progress, especially on the production side where the debate is characterized in a familiar and very American tension between tradition and modernism. One group, which I will loop loosely together as the "Digital First" movement, takes an almost Futurist approach to progress and

---

[9] Swensen, David and Schmidt, Michael, "News You Can Endow." *The New York Times* (Op-Ed), January 27, 2009. http://www.nytimes.com/2009/01/28/opinion/28swensen.html Accessed 10 Dec. 2011.
[10] Coll, Steve. "Think Tank: The Future of Journalism," *The New Yorker*, May 7 2009. http://www.newyorker.com/online/blogs/stevecoll/2009/05/the-future-of-journalism.html Accessed 10 Dec. 2011.

technology, abandoning traditional models in favor of total restructuring, seeking profit and sustainability as the ultimate goal. John Paton, the CEO of the Journal-Register Co., launched Digital First Media as a collaboration between his Journal-Register Co. and Media News Group, another newspaper company. Paton insists on a radical break from past models of production and profit, with maxims as incendiary as "our legacy business model is too costly," "traditional journalism is dead" and "as career journalists and managers we have entered a new era where what we know and what we traditionally do has finally found its value in the marketplace, and that value is about zero."[11]

Another loud voice, Clay Shirky, insists that news must be subsidized, cheap and free in order to serve the citizenry effectively.[12] Known for his energetic diatribes, TED talks and appearance in the documentary *Page One: Inside the New York Times and the Future of Journalism*, Shirky, like his Digital First peers, believes that "any way of creating news that gets cost below income, however odd, is a good way, and any way that doesn't, however hallowed, is bad."[13] Shirky's tendency to embrace new technology wholeheartedly has incurred criticism from the other camp, largely made up of career journalists and those focused on improving the quality of news over its accessibility or flashiness. Similarly, Alan Rusbridger, editor-in-chief of Guardian News & Media in the United Kingdom, received

---

[11] Paton, John, "WAN IFRA International Newsroom Summit: How the Crowd Saved Our Company," *Digital First*, Jun 8 2011. http://jxpaton.wordpress.com/2011/06/08/wan_ifra/ Accessed 10 Dec. 2011.
[12] Shirky, Clay. "Why We Need the News Environment to Be Chaotic," *Clay Shirky*, July 9 2011. http://www.shirky.com/weblog/2011/07/we-need-the-new-news-environment-to-be-chaotic/ Accessed 10 Dec. 2011.
[13] Shirky, "Why We Need the News Environment to Be Chaotic"

immediate flack from his peers when Guardian media went "digital first," putting resources and attention into a digital model and foregoing not only a print-focused model but also traditional story forms and reporting processes.

Those career journalists in resistance to the Digital First crowd aren't dinosaurs, but rather focus their concerns on quality over sustainable profit, and often raise the argument of journalism as a public good rather than a network of media corporations. Tom Matlack, writer and former CFO for The Providence Journal Co., emphasizes our society's "collective disgust at mixing business with journalism,"[14] while Pulitzer-Prize winning journalist Steve Coll, in a *New Yorker* column, found Shirky's claims to be on the right track but missing the real threat "to the values and practice of independent, professional journalism as we have known it since the nineteen-sixties or so."[15] Coll does not outright defend the "old" way, but insists that society critically examine what irreplaceable good, if any, traditional journalism provides, and if it is worth protecting.

Dean Starkman, an editor at *Columbia Journalism Review,* outright criticized the Digital First crowd, calling their vision for the future "anti-institutional," "ahistorical," and "hazy at best," taking issue not with the restructuring of the news business but with the group's "light regard for journalism itself."[16] This begins to get at yet another side of the issue: the personal nature that

---

[14] Matlack, Tom, "The Rebirth of Newspapers," *The Huffington Post*. May 18, 2011. http://www.huffingtonpost.com/tom-matlack/ny-times-paywall-_b_863745.html Accessed 12 Nov 2011.
[15] Coll, Steve. "Think Tank: It's About the Journalism," *The New Yorker*, March 16 2009. http://www.newyorker.com/online/blogs/stevecoll/2009/03/its-about-the-j.html Accessed 10 December 2011.
[16] Starkman, Dean. "Confidence Game: The Limited Vision of the News Gurus," *Columbia Journalism Review*, Nov/Dec 2011. http://www.cjr.org/essay/confidence_game.php Accessed 10 Dec 2011.

drives this conflict, an erosion of trust between the old and the new that Jay Rosen, another Digital First supporter, calls "fucking neurotic."[17] Rosen points to the sharp split between traditional news reporters and bloggers, or "we interactive people," as a major divide in production method but also in the conception of what "news" really is.

I chronicle all of this disruption and experimentation to illuminate the amount of upheaval in today's news industry and the broad variety of "solutions" proposed by different parties. At best, there is only a recent consensus towards increasing the focus on the consumer and towards using technology to achieve this end. At this time, as consumer-oriented news movements like Digital First hone their product and structure, and as newsroom managers grow more comfortable with the benefits of technology and social media, more newsrooms finally embrace the opportunity of the digital age than oppose it.

As Ken Paulson, former *USA Today* editor and current president and CEO of the American Society of News Editors, put it, "Instead of getting beat up by new technology, [news organizations] are beginning to exploit it for very positive ends."[18] This is partly because producers are now tapping into what could create demand for an improved journalistic product and looking more closely at what the American news consumer wants and needs.

---

[17] Rosen, Jay. "The Psychology of Bloggers vs. Journalists: My Talk at South by Southwest." *PressThink.org*, March 12, 2011. http://pressthink.org/2011/03/the-psychology-of-bloggers-vs-journalists-my-talk-at-south-by-southwest/ Accessed 10 Dec. 2011.
[18] Paulson, Ken. Interview by Caroline Klibanoff. Digital film recording. The Newseum, Washington, D.C., Dec. 6 2011.

Consumers Choose the News

This third area of focus, the consumer- and citizen-driven model, draws upon free market politics and the interactive, fast-paced Internet landscape to seek areas of improvement and growth in journalism. It is not without its critics – McChesney mentions in his introduction that "the notion that all we citizens need to do is sit back and relax and let the free market and digital technologies work their magic is increasingly unconvincing" – but more and more, scholars, critics and news managers are discovering the inevitable strength of user demand and the importance of serving the news to the people in the best way possible.[19] The "Digital First" community calls it "The Crowd," and recognizes the immense power of the masses in a digital age: "The crowd collectively knows more about any subject, city or event we choose to cover than we do. Armed with the same tools – and in many cases – equal access to information and the search capabilities to provide history and context, the Crowd can do what we do."[20] Tom Matlack, like many career journalists, sees the public as responsible customers: "You [readers] just have to demand, and be willing to pay for, a news product worthy of your affections."[21] Despite the arguments over the details of this model, there is a consensus that the demands, abilities and desires of news consumers are not to be overlooked; thus we see the link between economically prosperous news sources, quality journalism, and

---

[19] McChesney x
[20] Paton, "WAN IFRA International Newsroom Summit: How the Crowd Saved Our Company."
[21] Matlack, "The Rebirth of Newspapers."

satisfied, informed consumers—those readers, watchers, listeners and fully-immersed media *hubs* who make up today's audience for news.

Leading this line of reasoning is *Reuters* and *Slate* media reporter Jack Shafer, who very clearly holds the reader liable for the news available to them: "I prefer to blame news consumers for journalism's deficiencies," he says. "Readers and viewers aren't as critical about their favorite news outlets as they should be, except to complain that *The New York Times* isn't as liberal as it should be or that Fox has failed to terminate the career of Barney Frank."[22]

Jeff Jarvis is a professor in journalism at the City University of New York and a media consultant known for his book, *Public Parts: How Sharing in the Digital Age Improves the Way We Work and Live*.[23] As is evident from his book title, Jarvis is a fierce believer in the power of the Internet to bring together consumers to demand better products and service, especially in journalism. He blogs at his personal site, Buzz Machine, about trends in the news industry and shines a spotlight on the changes reflecting consumer intervention, especially instances where consumers demand improvement in news production, i.e. seeking better fact-checking or exploring privacy policies for subscribers. A third voice from this angle is blogger Alan Mutter, a consumer-as-agents enthusiast with the benefit of a lifetime spent weathering the changes of technology in journalism as a reporter, editor, start-up director and new media consultant.

---

[22] Shafer, Jack. "Media bias? Give me more, please!" *Reuters*, Sept. 20 2011. http://blogs.reuters.com/jackshafer/2011/09/20/media-bias-give-me-more-please/ Accessed 10 Dec. 2011.
[23] Jarvis, Jeff. *Public Parts: How Sharing in the Digital Age Improves the Way We Work and Live*. New York: Simon & Shuster, 2011. Print.

Consumer-centered thinking is a meeting place for the various arguments that shape today's debate, and so it follows that this is the most important zone in which to place resources and focus as we move forward in this century. It is precisely where Digital First leaders and legacy journalists come together, where a peace is made between journalism that serves the public at large (i.e. a public good) and that which serves the paying customer, and where government and journalists work together to determine the best possible future outcome for news producers and citizens alike.

Information Needs of a Changing Audience

Much of the existing discussion establishes that the demands of consumers will prove to be effective currency for mandating change in journalism production, along the lines of what consumers want and need (i.e. free-market determination). The question then becomes: what *do* consumers want and need in a news product, and does it differ from what the general public "needs" from its press, as the Fourth Estate of American democracy? Further, does a more critical, media-savvy and informed public have different demands than a less news-literate one?

The literature on the desires and behavior of news consumers frequently crosses into non-journalistic territory because so many of the changes that affect modern news readers carry over to those readers' social, work and recreation habits. The Pew Research Center's Internet and American Life Project released a report in 2010 called "Understanding the Participatory Consumer: How Internet and Cell

Phone Users Have Turned News Into a Social Experience," making a valid and interesting sociological case on modern behavior, but not one that edges any closer to a defined problem or solution for improving news specifically.[24]

The literature on the needs of the public is more relevant and practical, but these reports tend to resist placing any agency with the common user despite the fact that the modern media landscape is rife with empowered, free agent individuals. 2007 marked the launch of the Knight Commission on the Information Needs of Communities in a Democracy, a project intended to assess the needs of the modern news consumer. This offered a slightly more niche angle, and certainly a more citizen-oriented one, than the Pew Project for Excellence in Journalism's annual State of the News Media Report, and focused on finding solutions where the Pew report focused on the dire circumstance of news profitability. In 2009, Knight-Aspen published "Informing Communities: Sustaining Democracy in the Digital Age" (with a participant list that reads like a Who's Who in Modern Media, including Jeff Jarvis, John Carroll, Madeleine Albright, Jon Leibowitz, Craig Newmark, Marissa Mayer, and Walter Isaacson) a report that concluded, "the time has come for new thinking and aggressive action to dramatically improve the information opportunities available to the American people, the information health of the country's communities and the information vitality of our democracy."[25] The

---

[24] Purcell, Kristen et al, "Understanding the Participatory News Consumer," Pew Research Center Project for Excellence in Journalism, March 1, 2010. http://www.pewInternet.org/~/media/Files/Reports/2010/Understanding%20the%20Participatory%20News%20Consumer.pdf Accessed 10 Dec. 2011.

[25] Knight Commission on the Information Needs of Communities, *Informing Communities: Sustaining Democracy in the Digital Age*. The Aspen Institute: Washington, D.C. 2009. http://www.knightcomm.org Accessed 10 Dec 2011. PDF.

report suggested different models "that will support the kind of journalism that has informed Americans," including a hyper-local focus, different payment systems, and perhaps most interestingly for my question, an independent non-profit called the Media Standards Trust that ensures quality in news on behalf of the public.[26] These examples are a representative of the whole; all of the proposed plans from the 2009 report placed the onus of responsibility upon news producers, to better serve a remote and passive public. While a watershed report in many ways, "Informing Communities" still fell into the trap of construing the American public as helpless and incapable of acting in its own best interest.

In 2011, the Federal Communication Commission's similarly-titled report, "The Information Needs of Communities," improves this type of study as it pursues the idea that today's public is neither remote nor passive, but highly engaged and participatory. The FCC examines all aspects of information sharing in the digital age, the public media sphere, and the effect the Internet has had on community relations. It acknowledges the discrepancy, arisen in recent years, between the many ways to get a wide variety of fast, cheap news, and the still-persistent loss of accountable, professional, and local reporting, arguing that the benefits of digital news have not been enough to overcome "gaps in coverage," creating "media deficits in many communities."[27] (It is hard to imagine today's world having anything to do with a "media deficit," but the report identifies a deficit of quality content, not

---

[26] Informing Communities 5, 40
[27] Waldman, Steven and the Working Group on Information Needs of Communities. *The Information Needs of Communities: The Changing Media Landscape in a Broadband Age.* Federal Communications Commission, July 2011. www.fcc.gov/infoneedsreport, 7

outlets or modes of information sharing.) The report concludes that current media regulations are not in concordance with the information needs of communities, and that the FCC must re-assess its role in serving digital consumers.

And so while the FCC's vision for ensuring a healthy future for American journalism lies in policy reform and government oversight, mine lies fully in the realm of the empowered, educated consumer. I agree with the basis of the FCC's proposal—that improved transparency on the part of government and the media can "remove obstacles to innovation,"—but, based on my analysis of the Information Needs report, I do not find that government policy is sufficient or even terribly relevant to an immediate, on-the-ground impact on journalism. In my view, the gap between the media and the government (i.e. FCC regulation over information dissemination) continues to grow, while citizens become the primary driving force in determining how news outlets profit and succeed, as has traditionally happened in the free market. That being said, the report's overarching goal is in line with my own: "Ignoring the ailments of [media] will mean that serious harm may be done to our communities – but paying attention to them will enable Americans to develop, literally, the best media system the nation has ever had."[28]

The Information Needs of Communities report benefits from its recent data; on the contrary, a 2003 report by the American Press Institute, "We Media," targets a more apt solution but is dated. We Media offers an in-depth look at the historical importance of the news consumer, from the ideological conception in 1995 by

---

[28] Waldman, *The Information Needs of Communities*, 15

Nicholas Negroponte, to the on-the-ground implications in 2003 when the report was published.²⁹ Because the landscape of journalism, and the Internet for that matter, is vastly different today than it was in 2003, this report primarily serves my purposes as a historical survey. It is essential to see what concerns dominated the conversation nine years ago in order to make sense of today's world. The report frequently dates itself (most notably with a section titled "Weblogs Come of Age,") and yet We Media is extremely forward thinking, providing a good model for the goals of this paper. To complete the report, the research team targeted "people from the future," like early adopters to new technology, and this tactic worked. We Media accurately predicts the state of journalism in 2011, an era of "two-way journalism" where "the audience becomes not consumers, but pro-sumers, a hybrid of consumer and producer."ⁱ They predict that by 2021, "citizens will produce 50 percent of the news peer-to-peer."³⁰ Interestingly, Dan Gillmor, who now associates with the Digital First group, wrote the foreword to We Media including a line echoing (or perhaps scooping) his peers Paton and Shirky: "My readers know more than I do. This has become almost a mantra in my work. It is by definition the reality for every journalist…and it's a great opportunity, not a threat…if modern American journalism has been a lecture, it's evolving into something that incorporates a conversation."³¹

---

[29] Bowman, Shayne and Willis, Chris. "We Media: How Audiences Are Shaping the Future of News and Information," The Media Center at The American Press Institute, Sept. 21 2003. http://www.hypergene.net/wemedia/weblog.php Accessed 22 Oct. 2011.
[30] Bowman, "We Media," Introduction
[31] Bowman, "We Media," Introduction

We Media is a futuristic and perceptive collection of information, but also frustratingly poses the same questions we debate today: who defines good journalism? Who protects its integrity? And who holds the most power, news producers or news consumers? We Media goes as far as to identify the rise of "participatory journalism," a bottom-up model where citizens are actively involved and integrated in the news production and consumption processes, but does not grapple with the implications of such a change.[32] That appears to be our problem in 2012: dealing with a new form of audience that is at once the Achilles heel of modern journalism and its potential savior.

Media Literacy: A Savvier Pro-Sumer

If the consumer is the primary determining factor of how, what, and where we gather news in the future, as all of these reports ultimately indicate, then we must insist on a smart consumer, one that makes choices in his or her best interest and in the interests of the greater community. In the last twenty years, movements to improve American media literacy (fluency and adaptability across technology platforms and the Internet) have dominated the conversation in this arena. "Media literacy" is generally understood as a fluency that encompasses the whole of digital media, especially entertainment; news literacy is regarded as a branch of media literacy, focusing more narrowly on comprehension of news, journalism and verified information in the digital age.

---

[32] Bowman, "We Media," Chapter 1

Media literacy initiatives have technically been around since Marshall McLuhan's theorizing, though only in their modern form—that is, pursuing improved media literacy through classroom education – since the early 1990s.[33] The Aspen Institute appears to have gone down the media literacy road briefly and then abandoned it; in 1993, Patricia Aufderheide published "A Report of the National Leadership Conference on Media Literacy," with such literacy defined as "the ability of a citizen to access, analyze and produce information for specific outcomes."[34] Similarly, a 1998 collection of essays, *The Public Voice in a Democracy at Risk*, highlights the attempt at closing the gap between the citizenry, the government, and the press through "civic journalism," an attempt to "improve the press' contribution to the quality of public life…to stimulate more informed citizen participation in public business and raise the quality of public deliberation."[35]

And yet over the years, one voice has remained most invested and prominent in the media literacy field – that of Renee Hobbs, who authored a chapter in *The Public Voice* asking the following questions: "What kinds of knowledge, attitudes, and skills are essential for being a citizen in a media age? How do we create opportunities for young people to develop their interests in democracy? What role

---

[33] Powers, Elia, "Teaching News Literacy in the Age of New Media: Why Secondary School Students Should be Taught to Judge the Credibility of the News they Consume," Master's Dissertation, Washington University in St. Louis, August 2010. PDF, 10.
[34] Aufderheide, Patricia. "Media Literacy: A Report of the National Leadership Conference on Media Literacy," Aspen Institute, Communications and Society Program, 1993. http://eric.ed.gov/ERICWebPortal/search/detailmini.jsp?_nfpb=true&_&ERICExtSearch_SearchValue_0=ED365294&ERICExtSearch_SearchType_0=no&accno=ED365294. Accessed 20 Oct. 2011.
[35] Salvador, Michael and Sias, Patricia ed. The *Public Voice in a Democracy at Risk*. Westport, CT: Praeger, 1998. Accessed via Google Books 14 Jan 2012, 115.

can the media, teachers and parents play?"[36] She references Aufderheide's Aspen report and reduces media literacy to manageable terms: awareness of time and choice in media consumption, critical reading, viewing and production skills, analysis of the political and cultural context of the media environment, and media advocacy. In *The Public Voice,* Hobbs addresses the challenges of implementing media literacy curriculum in a public education system already rife with problems of its own, and the outpacing of technological advancement against educational materials, and cites the need for media literacy education to take place in schools to reach a broad cross-section of the population. It is remarkable how many of her original claims still resonate today, fourteen years after publication, and how directly her ideas play into the news literacy movement.[37]

Hobbs continues her scholarship on this topic today, notably in an indispensable 2010 white paper published in collaboration with the Aspen Institute and the Knight Foundation called "Digital and Media Literacy: A Plan of Action," which very explicitly details the steps needed to enact greater media literacy across the American citizenry, as well as the impact such an educational change may have.[38] She has also authored a number of books, including *Digital and Media Literacy: Connecting Culture and Classroom, Reading the Media: Media Literacy in High School English,* and *Copyright Clarity: How Fair Use Supports Digital Learning,* and is co-editor of the *Journal for Media Literacy Education.* Just as in

---

[36] Salvador, *The Public Voice,* 58
[37] Salvador, *The Public Voice,* 59
[38] Hobbs, Renee. "Digital and Media Literacy: A Plan of Action," A White Paper. The Aspen Institute Communications and Society Program, 2010. PDF.

news literacy, educational initiatives remain the focus of the media literacy movement, anchored by an in-depth 2007 report by the National Association for Media Literacy Education, and face many of the same challenges in this arena. Hobbs proves to be a key critical voice in my assessment of news literacy initiatives as so many of the existing programs mirror the media literacy trajectory, especially through secondary education.

News Literacy Education

Given the focus on improving the consumer base and the efforts already made on behalf of media literacy, it is not surprising that many journalists have begun to look to news literacy education as a potential savior for the future of news. The implication of nearly all the literature on media and news literacy is that consumers must be *taught* to act in their own best interests. Journalists care about the quality of news, and the government cares about the quality of news, but there is no natural mandate that consumers *must* care, outside of the obvious democratic pitfalls that would ensue. As Jack Shafer puts it, "Journalism can only be as good as the readers that consume it. When they stop caring about its quality, it's gonna be lights out for journalism."[39] The obvious solutions are engagement and education, with the best option being a combination of the two that could lead to future generations of voracious, well-informed news consumers, a democracy's dream.

---

[39] Shafer, Jack. "Why Media Bias Isn't a Journalistic Problem," open interview moderated by Mallary Jean Tenore. Online Chat, Poynter.org, Sep. 21 2011 http://www.poynter.org/latest-news/top-stories/146685/live-chat-today-with-jack-shafer-why-media-bias-isnt-a-journalistic-problem/

News literacy education groups, like the News Literacy Project in Bethesda, Md., and the Center for News Literacy in Stony Brook, New York, appear to align themselves somewhere between the Digital First movement's embrace of technology and consumer choice, and Hobbs' emphasis on instilling the necessary checks and balances in youth through education in order to create an informed, savvy consumer class with the ability to deconstruct the news and adapt rapidly to new technology.

Dean Miller, founder of the Stony Brook Center for News Literacy (one of two central institutions in this movement) wrote a 2010 column in *The Christian Science Monitor* claiming the benefit to journalism from a more news-literate public, and positing his program as part American civics course, part critical thinking skills, and part media-savvy education. Miller implores established journalists to come teach their skills to the public: "Come work among the consumers for a while…this is a course an old-school journalist can teach surprisingly well." His proposal demands immediate action and takes into account the power of consumer-driven media: "Citizens armed with the power of discernment will do more to rescue journalism than any dozen panel of veteran editors ruminating about their golden years in power and musing about better business models."[40]

Because the need to educate consumers has only been realized of late as the primary stake in 2012's media landscape, the literature on such is at best very recent and minimal, and at worst, absent from the discussion. The current schemes to increase news literacy are almost all classroom- and curriculum-based, with a

---

[40] Miller, Dean. "Want Better Journalism? Boost News Literacy," *The Christian Science Monitor*. Stony Brook, NY, Jan. 14 2010. Print.

few instances of education taking place in the gaming and social media sphere, but critical study of any these programs is mostly nonexistent because they are so new. Yet, it is precisely this "in-beta" nature that makes it so crucial to study news literacy programs at this time.

In terms of critical assessment, news literacy advocacy groups and funding groups conduct their own post-course testing, and some discussion lives among media minds like Gillmor and Clay Johnson, author of *The Information Diet*, as to the end results of systematic, large-scale news literacy education. Johnson in particular stresses a deep concern about information overload and how we might become "healthier" consumers. He draws a useful parallel to America's food and obesity problem: that our struggle isn't that we consume too much information, but that we live among an overabundance of "junk" information that cheapens our quality of life and lowers our efficiency, and so must discipline ourselves to maintain a high-quality information diet. Instead of blaming the media companies that proliferate wild opinion and noise, or the government for not policing it better, he sees the demand for "junk information" as the root of the problem; "we are what we consume."[41] And yet, Johnson offers few solutions, probably because there are no obvious ones, this being the chronic plague of news literacy programs; self-discipline and awareness of poor choices can only take one so far.

Johnson is embedded in the radical open-source movement, having served as

---

[41] Eaves, David. "Not Brain Candy: A Review of *The Information Diet* by Clay Johnson." *Eaves.ca,* Dec. 15, 2011. http://eaves.ca/2011/12/15/not-brain-candy-a-review-of-the-information-diet-by-clay-johnson/ Accessed 13 Jan. 2012.

director of Sunlight Labs, which works to make the U.S. government more transparent and accountable through demanding open-source documents and data. Open-source (liberating the Internet's code and data), open-government (liberating documents and increasing transparency) and open-news (destroying the old hierarchical divide between news producers and consumers) movements may be considered fringe at this time, but are becoming increasingly influential and play directly into the empowerment of the individual and the need for news literacy. The Knight-Mozilla collaboration I mentioned earlier focuses its operations on open-source Web coding, new application development and data journalism.[42] Along the same lines, since 2009 the grassroots "Hacks/Hackers" organization has connected journalists and technologists in networking, conference and social settings to re-imagine the future of news and information.[43] All of these mergers between technology and journalism breed innovation and smartly focus on the consumer's needs, but still tend to place the consumer as secondary to the producer in terms of responsibility and agency. The news literacy movement no doubt supports the ideals and innovative nature of the open news movement, but the focus of news literacy is to educate the consumer for *whatever* the future news landscape looks like – to possess critical thinking skills and be able to flex them, navigating an information deluge in any IT climate.

---

[42] "*The New York Times* joins Mozilla and Knight Foundation to Drive Open Innovation in News," *Mozilla* blog, March 9 2012. http://blog.mozilla.com/blog/2012/03/09/new-york-times-joins-mozilla/ Accessed 19 March 2012.
[43] Hacks/Hackers "About." *Hacks/Hackers* blog, 2010. http://hackshackers.com/about/

Further, there is still no consensus on the method for better educating news consumers. Between Sunlight Labs, Data.gov, Knight-Mozilla and Digital First's open newsroom philosophy, the shared idea is to democratize access to information and resources, and increase the public's power to use that information to work towards a better society. The major difference comes into play in the practical approach: where Johnson and open-source advocates seek solutions in code, data and the Internet, news literacy initiatives usually work through the more traditional avenue of compulsory education.

Working through schools to increase news literacy has its own difficulties, best examined by Elia Powers, a young journalist and preeminent news literacy scholar who wrote his Masters thesis at Washington University in St. Louis on the need to expand news literacy curriculum in secondary schools. His paper gives an important run-down of the barriers to increasing news literacy curriculum in the public education system, the ways to overcome them and adjusting news literacy education to fit state standards. According to Powers, secondary schools are the ideal place to impart the tenets of news literacy because of the critical, formative age of those students "particularly prone to undervalue access to reliable news" and because of the mass-market approach, that embedding news literacy lessons in the existing education system pushes the curriculum to a broad swath of the population.[44] Yet, modifying state-mandated school curriculum is never an easy

---

[44] Powers, "Teaching News Literacy," 2

task on the sheer basis of bureaucracy and resistance to change. Powers identifies the primary challenges:

    a) Competition for class time among initiatives like STEM and No Child Left Behind
    b) Lack of teacher and parent familiarity with the news literacy movement
    c) Political sensitivities in teaching news literacy
    d) Inadequate classroom access to relevant media technology

To address this, news literacy developers attempt to shape curricula to better suit state critical reading or civics standards, so that teachers can incorporate news literacy materials more seamlessly at no expense to other subjects. And yet a lack of resources for lesson plans and teacher training persists as an obstacle to states embracing news literacy as part of the required curriculum, with lawmakers deciding that they cannot require teachers to include lessons on unfamiliar subjects.[45] Thus, out of necessity, the still-green news literacy movement has become a grassroots force, what Powers calls a "bottom-up" approach that brings individual educators, journalists, school administrators and community members on board, directing micro-size efforts that are more powerful on a small scale than a blanket educational policy that may never get off the ground.[46] Alan Miller, president and CEO of the News Literacy Project, agrees with this approach, and it is evident from the Stony Brook Center for News Literacy that they agree as well, given the nature of their teaching-the-teachers model. While Stony Brook and the NLP may be powerhouses of potential change with sufficient funding and resources, news literacy has not yet arrived on the national consciousness. As Frederick

---

[45] Powers, "Teaching News Literacy," 48
[46] Powers, "Teaching News Literacy," 60

Blevens, a Stony Brook-trained professor using the Center's model at Florida International University, puts it, "Most of us are out here, lonely little merchants [of news literacy] at our universities trying to scrape up a few courses... it's the difference between running an experiment in an ideal laboratory and trying to mix your chemicals in a shot glass."[47]

This grassroots nature of the news literacy movement showcases just how young this area of study is – which means that to some extent, any hard and fast conclusions drawn about the current models are premature, and so assessment of news literacy programs should be as malleable and fluid as the subject itself. At the same time, critical evaluation is needed to determine how to best move forward, which is why I pursue this close analysis of the News Literacy Project's current operations in schools, taking into account the greater context that shaped this development. The Information Needs of Communities report included a brief discussion of digital, media and news literacy at the end of the report, begging the question as to why the rest of the report focused so heavily on supply-side solutions if it's true that "what citizens demand will affect not only democracy but the dynamics of the media market."[48] The report notes that news literacy used to be a common fixture in American education but has taken a dive in the wake of more violent or provoking news reports, and cites the News Literacy Project as evidence of hope in changing this, but does not pursue a closer look at the NLP's operations.

---

[47] Loth, Renee. "Teaching News Literacy in the Digital Age," *The Chronicle Review*. Feb. 5, 2012. http://chronicle.com/article/Teaching-News-Literacy-in-the/130613/?sid=cr&utm_source=cr&utm_medium=en Accessed 8 March 2012.

[48] The Information Needs of Communities, 220

Criticism of news literacy education so far has centered on the journalistic root and emphasis of these programs: that journalists aren't equipped to teach, that the curriculum is developed by journalists desperate to protect the reputation and value of their profession, and that it romanticizes the ideals of journalism rather than recognizing the realities of modern journalism. In an interesting twist, while many of the media literacy goals align with those of news literacy, and while the two fields share the same approach (through secondary education) the most aggressive criticism of news literacy initiatives comes from Renee Hobbs herself. Hobbs' provocative article in *Nieman Reports* titled "News Literacy: What Not To Do" makes a solid argument in pointing out the potential pitfalls of a blanket education program designed and promoted by journalists on behalf of their own trade, and wisely cautions against any blind praise of American journalism: "The bottom line is if a news literacy course leaves students feeling frustrated that American journalistic practices do not meet the idealistic vision we have for journalism as a watchdog on power and a catalyst to democracy, that's OK."[49] It appears media literacy and news literacy advocates are faced with protecting their own distinct mission in a world of limited resources and tolerance for reform, especially since they share the education space. It could be that these two groups will join forces someday and ally to improve consumer education in the digital arena, but as of now the current divide between the two camps persists.

---

[49] Hobbs, Renee. "News Literacy: What Not to Do," *Nieman Reports Summer 2011 Online Exclusives.* Summer 2011. http://www.nieman.harvard.edu/reportsitem.aspx?id=102645 Accessed 10 Dec 2011.

Luckily, there is little debate that an informed citizenry is essential for American democracy to flourish. This has inhabited national awareness for many years, and has always gone hand-in-hand with access to quality news. As Powers notes, President Barack Obama stated in 2010:

> "Today's 24/7 echo-chamber amplifies the most inflammatory sound bites louder and faster than ever before. And it's also, however, given us unprecedented choice ...That's why we need a vibrant and thriving news business that is separate from opinion makers and talking heads. That's why we need an educated citizenry that values hard evidence and not just assertion."[50]

The vision of an ideal citizen—an engaged, aware consumer who reads, watches, comments, re-blogs, and rejects the news with an active eye for accuracy, fairness, and quality – is widely accepted, but existing literature varies in terms of *how* to achieve such an ideal (in-classroom education, extracurricular programs, open-newsroom transparency, reorganization of news sites) and in terms of *where* to focus efforts (on youth, social media start-ups, or teachers themselves).

Now that Powers has assessed the feasibility of implementing news literacy curricula into secondary education, and Hobbs has honed in on the potential landmines that such curricula might present, I will turn a critical eye on the same programs, gauging their effectiveness in creating a savvy consumer class capable of revaluing modern journalism. I will compare the current prototypes in education, and explore what possibilities might exist beyond the classroom.

---

[50] Obama, Barack. "Remarks by the President at University of Michigan Spring Commencement." Michigan Stadium, Ann Arbor, MI. 1 May 2010. Keynote address. Cited by Powers, 10.

CHAPTER 3: RESEARCH METHOD

Given the overarching context of a consumer-driven news media as the journalistic model of the 21st century, the goal of my research is to evaluate the news literacy education movement as a powerful force in developing a savvier news consumer base. I am interested in the implementation and results of news literacy education programs in public schools, particularly at the middle and high school level where it fits into existing curriculum in English, government, civics and journalism classes. Secondary school curriculum is a pertinent area of study for news literacy because many states recently revised their standards (particularly in civics and history) in the wake of dire reports released by the National Assessment Governing Board in the summer of 2011, and some of these redeveloped standards allow room for news literacy initiatives (or at the very least, media literacy initiatives).[51] Second, it makes sense to examine the news literacy education movement at the middle and high school levels because these are the generations that will, presumably, shape the future of American news media through participation in production or, more likely, through high levels of engagement and consumer demand.

---

[51] The National Assessment Governing Board, a division of the U.S. Department of Education, released a series of the Nation's Report Card in various subjects in the summer of 2011. While many results from these reports pointed towards an overall stagnation in test scores, the History and Civics reports were particularly alarming. Thus the question of education reform in these areas has reached national discourse. At the same time, the Common Core State Standards Initiative has redefined English and Math standards in 47 states so far to better align curriculum along a "common core." While no news literacy curriculum has been included in the standardization yet, there is evidence that among such disruption and reinvention that the new standards for public education will continue to change and develop. More information is available at www.corestandards.org and www.nationsreportcard.gov.

With that said, my research takes the form of a case study of the News Literacy Project's operations at Bethesda - Chevy Chase High School in Bethesda, Md. I will begin with an introduction to the NLP itself and a brief history of the program and similar others, and I will present the lay of the land in terms of major figures and organizations within this new, relatively small movement. I will then convey my experience observing the NLP in action at B-CC High School, through direct observation of the program in two classroom visits during which I took notes in a notebook and on my Macbook computer in Microsoft Word.

I began by reaching out to the NLP, since it is not only located near Washington but is one of two primary national news literacy organizations and the only one focused exclusively on middle school and high school. CEO Alan Miller and his staff were very receptive to my research plan and sent me material about the NLP and media literacy. I was able to interview Miller on the phone about the program's roots, operations and goals, and through Maureen Freeman, the D.C. Schools Coordinator for the NLP, I set up two visits to observe the program at B-CC High School. While the NLP has a number of operations in schools in New York City, Washington, D.C. and Chicago, B-CC High School presented an ideal opportunity because of its close location to where I live and the timing of the NLP's implementation there.

B-CC High School makes an interesting choice for a case study because it is part of the Montgomery County school district in Maryland, often referred to as a "model school system" for America with consistently high test scores, college acceptances and involved families. At the same time, affluent, high-performing suburban schools are growing scarcer in American public education, and so while B-CC High School may be a "model" school it does not accurately represent the majority of American high schools. The NLP also arranges for journalists to visit D.C. area charter schools like E.L. Haynes Public Charter, largely attended by students from disadvantaged socioeconomic backgrounds. The news literacy programming at such schools is different – essentially, there is more to teach, due to an overall lower literacy rate and less familiarity with news sources and production. To supplement my case study at B-CC High School, and upon Miller's recommendation, I also interviewed Eliza Ford, 8th grade literacy teacher at E.L. Haynes who has hosted the NLP in her classroom. This broadened my understanding of the NLP's programming and goals and the ways in which the curriculum must be modified to suit each school's particular audience. For additional background on the NLP I also spoke to the aforementioned Elia Powers regarding his news literacy dissertation.

    Outside of the NLP case study, I interviewed a number of media professionals to supplement my understanding of the news literacy landscape, including Emory journalism professor Sissel McCarthy. McCarthy, trained by the Center for News Literacy at Stony Brook, teaches news literacy in a college course that makes use of community service-based learning. After studying news literacy in McCarthy's undergraduate classroom, the college students then teach news literacy to students at a nearby middle school in Atlanta. I also communicated by email with Dean Miller and Howard Schneider of the Center for News Literacy at Stony Brook, two primary founders of the modern incarnation of news literacy education. They sent me additional resources and information and offered an interview if necessary, though my focus remained primarily on the NLP and youth education. Each interview was conducted by phone or in person, and I used a consent procedure and informed consent form to ensure that my participants understood the study and that they could contact me at any time.

For the case study at B-CC High School, my observation was based on the grounded theory approach developed by Glaser and Strauss, using inductive reasoning from case study data.[52] I selected the grounded theory approach primarily because of its roots in ethnography and the success the method has had in sociology, two disciplines that frame my work. Martyn Hammersly and Paul Atkinson offer a definition that pertains to my observational practice in *Ethnography: Principles in Practice*:

> In terms of data collection, ethnography usually involves the researcher participating, overtly or covertly, in people's daily lives for an extended period of time, watching what happens, listening to what is said, and/or asking questions through informal and formal interviews, collecting documents and artefacts – gathering whatever data are available to throw light on the issues that are the emerging focus of inquiry.[53]

At B-CC High School, I attended two fifty-minute classes served by the NLP, one English class and one Journalism class, in order to observe the possible difference in teaching news literacy in production-based (journalism) versus consumption-based

---

[52] Glaser, Barney G & Strauss, Anselm L. *The Discovery of Grounded Theory: Strategies for Qualitative Research*. Chicago: Aldine Publishing Company, 1967.
[53] Hammersly, Martyn and Atkinson, Paul. *Ethnography: Principles in Practice*, third edition. Routledge: London, 1983, 2007. Print, 3.

(English literature) classes. The same English teacher at B-CC High School taught both classes, lending some consistency to my research. Both classes were comprised of high-achieving juniors and seniors; the English class was Honors English 11, and the journalism class was Journalism 2, meaning students enrolled had already completed Journalism 1 with a minimum of one year's work for the high school newspaper, *The Tattler*. Each class was visited by a different journalist, and had different prior experiences with visiting journalists from the NLP, which I will detail in my case study.

Freeman and the NLP had set up all of the journalists' visits to the school, as well as my visit. I sat in the back of the classroom for each class, during *60 Minutes* producer Henry Schuster's visit to Honors English 11 and *Washington Post* reporter Lori Aratani's visit to Journalism 2. Before going to the school, I made a list of questions to ask should I get the opportunity to speak with anyone on the record, and key aspects of the program to look for, to better guide my observations. These questions covered: the purpose of news literacy education and whether or not that matched up with what I witnessed; the relationship between the classroom teacher and visiting journalist; the reactions and engagement level of the students; the effectiveness of the structure of the lesson plan; how a NLP visit compares to a regular lesson; the use of technology in NLP visits compared to non-NLP lessons; whether or not it was essential for a journalist to be present; the demographics of the classroom; the ease of news literacy curriculum implementation for the school, teacher, and students; the lesson taught for journalism versus English classes; what is being taught versus what is being learned; and reflections on the general classroom atmosphere. I used a digital tape recorder to record audio from each visit and later uploaded the recordings in MP3 format to my computer to transcribe. I wrote down my observations of the classes (from listening and watching) in a notebook as well as in a Microsoft Word document on my laptop. After each class, I wrote down my immediate reactions and findings to be able to recall them later.

I chose not to interview students in the program after reading many news articles that solicited opinions from students on news literacy education. I found the students' responses canned and not revealing of deeper reflection on news literacy education. I did, however, write down specific observations and quotes from students as I witnessed the NLP in action at B-CC High School. This choice to decline the voice of students in my research on a program that highlights the importance of youth agency and awareness may seem counterintuitive; however, as my findings reveal, student opinion already plays a minimal role in developing high school curriculum and the NLP is no exception. It is also difficult to isolate individual students for interviews that would be representative of a whole, since the spectrum of student interest, background and motivation is so broad even within these two classes. Thus, it is not surprising that student interviews rarely lead to revealing or insightful responses.

The interviews I conducted in addition to my case study helped frame my argument and offered essential context for me as a researcher, but for the reader to understand this case study within its historical and scholarly environment, additional information on the origins of the News Literacy Project will prove helpful. This is necessary for my conclusions as well. While Glaser and Strauss originally articulated a system of comparative analysis for qualitative data, Hammersly and Atkinson advise using a postmodern manifestation of the grounded theory approach developed by Adele Clarke called "situational analysis," which takes pragmatism and social complexity into consideration.[54] Because "theorizing [in ethnography] ought to involve an iterative process in which ideas are used to make sense of data, and data are used to change our ideas," it is important that I am able to contextualize the data I gathered and such "situational analysis" proves very useful in doing so.[55] Thus, I will begin with a "lay of the land" in news literacy education in order to provide context for my data.

---

[54] Hammersly and Atkinson, 167 citing Clarke, Adele. *Situational Analysis: Grounded Theory After the Postmodern Turn*. Thousand Oaks, CA: Sage, 2005.
[55] Hammersly and Atkinson, 159

CHAPTER 4: AN OVERVIEW OF NEWS LITERACY PROGRAMS

Origins of the News Literacy Movement

As revealed in my review of literature on the subject, news literacy education is a relatively new area of education reform and certainly a new area of scholarship in higher education. The origins of the movement can be traced to around 2007-2008, when the two most influential institutions of news literacy were founded – the News Literacy Project in Bethesda, Maryland and the Center for News Literacy in Stony Brook, New York. Though these organizations work together towards a common goal, they began independently and focus on different demographics. The Center for News Literacy focuses on journalists and college students, while the NLP focuses on middle school and high school youth.

The fact that both of these organizations cropped up independently at the same time reveals a distinct crisis point reached in 2008, when it became evident that the influx of news and information in the digital age presented certain challenges for news consumers. Certainly the first people to recognize the need for increased news literacy were journalists themselves, finding a public that devalued traditional journalism (evidenced by the massive departure of print subscriptions and advertisers, the move to blog and social media culture, and the attitude towards legacy media) and, tracing it to a lack of news literacy, to insufficient awareness of what makes a news report worth paying for.[56] In 2008 the Poynter Institute held a

---

[56] The devaluation of traditional journalism by the public is evident in a number of official reports and panels that detail this change, from the Knight Foundation's Commission on the Information Needs of Communities (panels, 2008 and 2009 and report, 2011) to a 2008 study by the Pew Research Center's Internet and American Life Project that details the shift to Internet published news, a decline in the use of news in classrooms and a declined interest in

conference called "Rebooting the News: Reconsidering an Agenda for American Civic Education" that declared news literacy a central focus for the year. The conference featured Howard Schneider, founder of the Center for News Literacy, and Renee Hobbs, among others.[57]

Concurrently, as mentioned in the literature review, the media literacy movement gained traction at this time, boosting the urgency for news literacy advocates and the legitimacy of their concerns. So, while the major and original figures in the news literacy movement are journalists or former journalists, as the awareness grows the movement finds support in other disciplines: academia, education, technology and web development, think tanks and research centers.

News literacy concepts and education initiatives are very malleable at this point, despite what some advocates may say, perhaps not wanting to reveal a lack of firm establishment. But the truth is that for all their benevolent work and careful, enthusiastic innovation, news literacy education programs are not yet widely embedded in the educational system or established as a common concept in American life, making it all the more pertinent to critically examine the existing programs and suggest improvements or addendums to improve the structure and implementation of these ideas. In fact, the newness and variability of news literacy education may perhaps be its greatest strengths in a society where traditionalism is found to be stagnant, and progress thrives in innovation, youth, and flexibility.

---

news among young people age 18-24. http://pewresearch.org/pubs/1066/Internet-overtakes-newspapers-as-news-source

[57] "Media Education Lab Convening October 23-25, 2008," *Youth Media Reporter* blog. 19 Sept 2008. http://www.youthmediareporter.org/2008/09/media_education_lab_convening.html. Accessed 6 March 2012.

The News Literacy Project

The News Literacy Project is the principal organization focused on news literacy education for grades six through twelve. Alan Miller, who worked as a Pulitzer Prize-winning investigative reporter for the *Los Angeles Times* for nearly 20 years, founded the NLP in 2008 upon seeing the need for young people to have greater access to resources on how to find credible information in today's information landscape. His observations at his daughter's middle school in Bethesda, Md. pointed to a lack of engagement with news media on the part of young people as well as a decline in the use of news in classrooms, leading him to seek a new way to "prepare students for their role as citizens at a time when it may be more needed than ever."[58] Because of this foundation in education, the News Literacy Project emphasizes its ability to fit into existing curriculum and supplement normal classroom lessons on critical reading and civics. It takes into account the digital age and the increased options presented to students in terms of news and information, and finds that "the nation's education system is not confronting this challenge [of myriad sources of greatly varying credibility] and the concept of news literacy is not widely discussed in public schools."[59] Since its founding the NLP has grown into a national organization with an impressive network and advisory board, and became a certified non-profit in 2012.

---

[58] The News Literacy Project. "About." *The News Literacy Project*. 2011. http://www.thenewsliteracyproject.org/about/
[59] The News Literacy Project: "About."

Miller leveraged his journalist network to bring together journalists and educators for the program, which now boasts an impressive roster of nearly 200 visiting journalists, though most have presented only two or three times each. Most are from major outlets, though a few are freelancers or bloggers for sites like ProPublica and TravelZoo. The NLP reached more than 2,000 students in 2011, expanding the program to a total of 21 middle schools and high schools in Chicago, New York City, and Washington D.C. [60] Outside the classroom, the NLP has initiatives to bring students into newsrooms in New York and Chicago, and to give students access to traditional newspapers donated by sponsors like *The New York Times* and *The Chicago Tribune*. The NLP also collaborates with the American Library Association and the Chicago Public Library to develop news literacy workshops, and hosts a number of public events with notable journalists to boost awareness of the program and its mission.

The structure of the News Literacy Project brings established journalists from a variety of media – television, newspaper, magazine, radio – into high school and middle school English, civics, government, history and journalism classes to work with students and discuss news literacy concepts. The choice to bring in journalists, instead of providing teachers with continuing education and news literacy materials, is rooted in the hope that the journalists' passion for their craft will be translated to students and that the novelty of a "guest speaker" approach

---

[60] The News Literacy Project. "Banner Year in 2011," *The News Literacy Project Blog.* Dec. 2011. http://www.thenewsliteracyproject.org/blog/the_news_literacy_project_concludes_a_banner_year_in_2011/ Accessed 13 Jan. 2012.

will engage students. In addition, the program makes use of technology like video, Skype, digital media and social media in presentations, thereby using the forms being discussed in a sort of meta-style proof of how important digital and news literacy are for a day-to-day existence. This model takes into account the recent decline of the Newspapers in Education program, a branch of the Newspapers Association of America that for years provided newspapers and journalistic resources to classrooms, but has struggled to meet the challenges of expense and digitization wrought by the digital age.[61]

According to the News Literacy Project's website, teachers and journalists are matched up according to subject matter: "A White House or city hall reporter might be a good fit for a government class, a former foreign correspondent might work well in a history class, and a feature writer could be ideal for an English class."[62] While the NLP operates in a few journalism classes, it targets students who are *not* in journalism classes, those who could be said to need news literacy education the most since they have less exposure to the craft of newsmaking. The program is strictly literacy, demonstrating how to become a better consumer of news – not intending to create future journalists, though "it aspires to light a spark of interest in consuming news and information that will make students better informed citizens and voters."[63]

---

[61] Powers, "Teaching News Literacy," 78-79
[62] The News Literacy Project. "Program." *The News Literacy Project.* 2011. http://www.thenewsliteracyproject.org/program
[63] The News Literacy Project, "Program."

There is not one news literacy curriculum, nor does the program supersede any curriculum already in place; instead "the highly adaptable NLP unit" is modified to fit a classroom's needs and schedule, usually delivered in six to ten classroom sessions, and the NLP encourages educators to use the unit as a way to meet state standards in critical reading and text analysis. The options are broad: the NLP has created a classroom guide with original lessons for use, but many visiting journalists prepare their own presentations based on current news or culture to relate to students, and teachers determine a final project suitable for the goals of the unit, where students either create a major journalistic piece (newspaper, video report, etc.) or a creative project (song, game, video) revealing the tenets of news literacy.[64]

An example of the NLP in action can be found in Eliza Ford's eighth grade literacy classroom at E.L. Haynes Public Charter School in Washington, D.C., a relatively new, year-round school in its fourth year of having a middle school and its second year of having an eighth grade. The school enrolls 800 students in kindergarten through ninth grade, with a student body that is 54% African-American, 25% Latino, 18% Caucasian and 3% Asian, with 62% of students qualifying for free or reduced lunch.[65] It is a high-performing charter school that students must apply to and be accepted in order to enroll.

Ford has taught at E.L. Haynes since 2008 and teaches literacy (Language Arts) and humanities, and is the sole representative for news literacy at the school.

---

[64] The News Literacy Project, "Program."
[65] E.L. Haynes Charter School, "About." 2011. http://www.elhaynes.org/aboutus.html

She worked with Alan Miller and the NLP to find a way to incorporate visiting journalists into her eighth grade curriculum and has found the experience overwhelmingly positive, as she now seeks to explore where else the NLP might fit into E.L. Haynes subject matter. In the fall, E.L. Haynes students in Ford's literacy class had a number of visits from the NLP "and the kids absolutely loved it," said Ford.[66] Compared to the two classes at B-CC High School, Ford's middle school students encompass a greater spectrum of abilities and knowledge, making it more difficult to import a pre-existing news literacy lesson without significant tailoring first. Her eighth graders span a third- to ninth-grade reading level, demonstrating that sometimes literacy is the first obstacle to news literacy in a charter school environment. However, she has found the NLP administration and visitors to be flexible and patient in working with her students' needs and the existing curriculum.

Ford finds that the goals of news literacy education help her students prepare for state assessments and fit in with D.C. curriculum, and she has seen increased analytical ability in her students' work post-NLP. The biggest challenge, unsurprisingly, is fitting news literacy in for the reasons Powers illuminated – lack of awareness among other teachers, the tenuousness of the classroom setting that is resistant to change, and finding time in a packed school year to dedicate to news literacy, despite how well it supports other educational goals. "I feel a lot of pressure time-wise," Ford said, which is why the flexible NLP unit appealed to

---

[66] Ford, Eliza. Interview by Caroline Klibanoff. Digital audio recording, March 8 2012. Phone.

her.[67] She could invite journalists in for a series of visits without incorporating the materials into every aspect of her curriculum (even though it is exactly this "part-time" attitude that I believe poses a barrier to true success for news literacy). Further, time constraints prevented her from much planning with visiting journalists beforehand, an idea I had highlighted as a potential area for improvement.

Ford does, however, see news literacy as a long-term goal and would like to incorporate it all year long; her approval of the program is especially notable because she does not come from a journalism background, demonstrating the ability of news literacy to "cross over" to non-journalistic realms as an area of utmost importance and urgency. "What they are trying to do is incredible," said Ford, "and what they are doing can continue to evolve and change and that's very important."

In 2008, NLP's financial supporters included the Knight Foundation, the Ford Foundation and Jim Cramer; in 2011, the list of donors was far longer, including some major educational foundations (Whitman High School Education Foundation, Charles H. Revson Foundation) but mostly journalistic ones (Gannett, The Chicago Tribune Company, The New York Times Company, HBO, AOL, Scripps Howard, Bloomberg LP, the David and Katherine Moore Family Foundation). Many of the individual donors are board members or journalists involved with the NLP. The biggest collaboration and support nationwide has come from the McCormick Foundation, which has a journalism-focused department.

---

[67] Ford, Eliza. Interview.

Mentioning the financial resources of the NLP is pertinent given that the harshest criticism of the program warns against a "by-journalists, for-journalists" agenda.[68] Yet, for the Washington, D.C. specific program, the San Diego wireless communications giant Qualcomm has led primary sponsorship. This alliance with a forward-thinking technology company provides great potential for moving news literacy education into the digital and social realm, though at this time Qualcomm is a supporter of in-classroom news literacy education. The News Literacy Project will make up the focus of my case study, for reasons stated in my Methods chapter.

The Center for News Literacy at Stony Brook

Howard Schneider, founding dean of Stony Brook University's School of Journalism, and Dean Miller, a former reporter and editor, direct the Center for News Literacy, largely funded by grants from the Knight Foundation and the McCormick Foundation. The Center, launched in 2007 within the Stony Brook School of Journalism, hosts a number of academic fellows each semester and primarily focuses on developing curriculum for teaching 10,000 undergraduates across all disciplines how to be more critical news consumers. Like the NLP, the Center does not believe it is sufficient to only train the next generation of journalists, but that news literacy is universally necessary, and Schneider insists the program "is not a cheerleading course for the press."[69] Miller concurs: "This isn't about reaching out to journalism majors. It's about preparing all students for full

---

[68] Hobbs
[69] Loth, Renee. "Teaching News Literacy in the Digital Age."

citizenship."[70] At Stony Brook, the news literacy course satisfies two core graduation requirements in humanities and history, and so far, has produced results according to some students.[71] Post-course testing revealed that "56 percent of students said they now verify stories before re-tweeting or linking to them, and 52 percent said they check out emails they receive before forwarding."[72]

The scale, as always, remains challenging; Schneider and his team aim to have reached their goal of 10,000 undergraduates by 2013, but they believe the curriculum needs to reach a much wider audience to make real change. Coming up against obstacles like a lack of awareness and limited time and funding, Stony Brook has used the grassroots method to try to spread the movement through training more teachers. The Center develops and promotes resources for teaching news literacy, including hosting training for news literacy teachers and publishing classroom materials that other teachers may use to emphasize news literacy in their own classrooms, including handouts, PowerPoints, and lesson plans. This training has led the "Stony Brook Method" to be implemented in about 100 secondary schools so far across the country.[73] It is a dynamic, engaging curriculum that includes a first-day assignment challenging students to tune out the news for 24 hours, a nearly impossible task that points directly to the importance of the course.

---

[70] Miller, Dean. "Want Better Journalism? Boost News Literacy."
[71] Loth, Renee. "Teaching News Literacy in the Digital Age"
[72] Loth, "Teaching News Literacy in the Digital Age"
[73] The Center for News Literacy, "Stony Brook Model." 2011. http://www.centerfornewsliteracy.org/?p=47

One example of successful teacher training is Sissel McCarthy, an instructor of journalism at Emory University and a longtime broadcast journalist with CNN and NBC. McCarthy learned the tenets and educational tools for teaching news literacy from the Center for News Literacy and implemented them in her Spring 2012 Emory course, *Journalism 260: News Literacy in a Digital Age*, for 32 undergraduate students, mostly non-journalism majors.[74] As the semester progressed and McCarthy used lectures, discussion and interactive exercises to impart the lessons of news literacy to her undergraduates, the college students then relayed what they learned to middle-school students at Coan Middle School in Atlanta, in a service-learning experience that spread the message of news literacy exponentially.

The lessons at Coan Middle School took place during regular classroom time in two eighth-grade Language Arts classes on four separate Fridays, for an hour per class each time. News literacy fits seamlessly into the "media studies" component of the Georgia state Language Arts curriculum, and McCarthy points out that many states that incorporate "media studies" into civics, social studies, or language arts classes do so because "it's really critical thinking skills, it's knowing how to analyze, evaluate and synthesize information, which are the three parts of critical thinking."[75] Emory University supported the course idea in keeping with its emphasis on liberal arts studies and critical thinking.

---

[74] The Center for News Literacy, "Emory University Launches News Literacy Course," *News*. March 2, 2012. http://www.centerfornewsliteracy.org/?p=1178

[75] McCarthy, Sissel. Interview by Caroline Klibanoff. MP3 Audio Recording, Caribou Coffee, Atlanta, Georgia. Jan. 8, 2012.

Because the tenets promoted by the NLP and Stony Brook are the same, a brief run-down of McCarthy's course content will provide important context for understanding and comparing my case study at B-CC High School, since it offers another example of how these ideas might be taught. McCarthy's students used materials from their own course to develop the middle-school curriculum in four areas, divided between the four weeks of classes. The first week tackled Information Neighborhoods, a common news literacy term to help readers distinguish between news, advertising, opinion and spam when so much of it is packaged similarly on digital platforms, and included the importance of verification, independence and sources. The second class covered the news process – who decides what the major stories are and who writes editorials – and looks more closely at the local newspaper. The third week used Harvard University's interactive Project Implicit game, which detects internal biases we subliminally possess to discuss the myth of objectivity. The fourth class was a truth and verification workshop, using real-life examples of falsified stories that made it to publication. The goal was to build the students' discernment skills and sense of healthy skepticism so that even years after the course, they could still deconstruct and contextualize the information deluge around them.

McCarthy plans to do pre- and post-class testing on her students, and noted that prior testing by Stony Brook has been positive. Students who had taken news literacy courses were more likely to vote and retained many of their verification skills one year later. And yet, the newness of the field prevents real progress from being evident at this time. As per Hobbs' criticism, the course makes it clear that American journalism is not always the best it can be (showing falsified news stories is one example), but strives to implicate consumers in that outcome, to develop a sense of responsibility for the press and an appreciation of the First Amendment.

The Center for News Literacy disseminates its educational materials through its website and through partnerships with other organizations, most notably the Newseum, the museum of news and the First Amendment in Washington, D.C. In addition to standard museum exhibits designed to educate and inform the public on the history and changing face of journalism, the Newseum has a "digital classroom" online operating in conjunction with the Center for News Literacy. The digital classroom provides news literacy materials for teachers and students through videos and the Newseum's presentation of the day's newspaper "Front Pages" from across the country; the website emphasizes the ways these lessons can match state educational standards in many areas.

The Center for News Literacy has also hosted two conferences on the subject that brought together interested parties. In 2009 stakeholders convened to bring news literacy to a national discussion and in 2011 to "develop strategies to speed the adoption and implementation of News Literacy, to improve the quality of the News Literacy curriculum, and to craft common assessment standards to better measure the impact of the curriculum on students."[76] Speakers included voices from across the news literacy and journalism spectrum, including Alan Miller of the

---

[76] Center for News Literacy, "Who? What? Why? Where? When? The Conference at a Glance," March 2011. http://newsliteracyconference.com/content/?page_id=1102

NLP, Dan Gillmor, Jeff Jarvis, David Folkenflik of NPR, Ken Auletta of *The New Yorker,* Tom Rosenstiel of the Pew Project for Excellence in Journalism, Paul Sparrow of the Newseum, and a number of people from the Center itself. These conferences have a relatively high profile and make it clear that the discussion of news literacy at this juncture revolves around its implementation in education (as opposed to another field like social media or extracurricular areas). The Center for News Literacy and the News Literacy Project are the two figureheads of this movement and work together on their goals, only differing slightly in their actual methodology (the NLP through classroom visits, the Center through teacher training) and target demographic (the NLP in grades six through twelve, the Center for all ages and specifically undergraduate students.)

News literacy initiatives outside the classroom

Despite the focus on youth and secondary education that has largely characterized the news literacy movement, there are some approaches that take into account the need for news literacy among all demographics – young and old alike – and the need for building strong, literate communities that thrive on a cycle of good information and good consumers. It is essential to look at these programs offered outside of the traditional secondary and higher education systems, since currently the significant news literacy discussion is limited to that realm.

I mentioned earlier the "open newsroom" system proffered by Digital First Media. This is a radical, experimental answer to consumer empowerment that literally invites readers into the newsroom physically or digitally to help produce the paper, and keeps meetings public and web-streamed, realizing that "Digital First really means Reader First or Community First."[77] This is a perfect example of where the news literacy argument fits in to the latest mergers between technology and journalism, and recalls We Media's 2003 prediction that "by 2012, citizens will produce 50 percent of the news peer-to-peer."[78] *The Register-Citizen*, a Digital First Media paper, not only emphasizes crowdsourcing and community fact-checking in its production technique, but also partners with local citizen blogs and local libraries, provides computers and editors for local bloggers, and built a classroom within the newsroom open to all in the hopes of making the newsroom a community center. In many ways, this represents a radical push forward to new territory, and yet it harkens back to the original newspaper-as-community-builder that small town papers once were. The classroom, and the paper's insistence on educating and including the public in the news process, is a landmark leap towards consumer-oriented, consumer-driven media without sacrificing quality, standards or profit.

A similar idea was instituted in October 2011 at *The Guardian*, which opted to open up its newslists of upcoming stories in the hopes that "readers were able to help newsdesks work out which stories were worth investing precious reporting resources in." To date, the paper still uses this experimental method, and feedback has ranged from moderate impact to high hopes for changed coverage according to

---

[77] "What the Newsroom Café taught us about improving local journalism," *Register Citizen Open Newsroom Project blog*. Sep. 13, 2011 http://newsroomcafe.wordpress.com/ Accessed 9 March 2012.
[78] We Media, Introduction

reader interest; the paper noted after a week that "whatever competitive advantage may have been lost by giving rivals a clue what we were up to was more than made up for by a growing range of ideas and tips from readers."[79]

This aligns more with the open news movement than the news literacy movement, though the two share many of the same goals and in fact one (news literacy) is quite necessary for the other to work. Ideally the future will hold collaboration between these two fields. The major players in the open government movement come directly from journalism and many overlap with the news literacy movement. For example, Kathy Kiely, managing editor of the Sunlight Foundation and a longtime journalist, has led many presentations in schools for the NLP.[80]

Another significant effort has developed in giving consumers the tools to evaluate web information on the Web itself, through better fact-checking technology (by man or machine). The biggest advocate in this sector is Craig Newmark, best known as the founder of Craigslist.org. Newmark serves on the boards of both the News Literacy Project and the Sunlight Foundation, as well as the board of the Center for Public Integrity, and he is one of many who believe that a major flaw in today's news environment is a lack of verified facts. Building off existing, independent fact-checking groups like PolitiFact, Factcheck.org and American Public Media's Public Insight Network, and tech advancements like an automatic

---

[79] Inside the Guardian Blog, "Lessons from our Open News Trial," *The Guardian UK*. Oct. 17, 2011. http://www.guardian.co.uk/help/insideguardian/2011/oct/17/guardian-newslist Accessed 9 March 2012.

[80] The Sunlight Foundation in Washington, D.C. operates a number of individual departments working towards open data and open source government, including Sunlight Labs (web development), Sunlight Reporting (journalism) and the original Sunlight Foundation which works with government agencies. More information is available at www.sunlightfoundation.com

"truth goggle" fact-checking application, Newmark wants to see a network of citizen and professional fact-checkers who essentially patrol the Internet and contribute to a better schema of judgment for news, along reliable/unreliable axes. His idea is theoretical at this time, but his determination is contagious; as he noted, "This is the biggest thing I might help with in my life."[81] Newmark has spoken extensively about developments in journalism and technology and most of his arguments can be traced back to his insistence on a news-literate public. On his website, CraigConnects, he divides his attention into six categories: Back-to-Basics Journalism, Public Diplomacy, Consumer Protection, Technology for the Common Good, Open Government, and Military Families, the first five of which directly incorporate news literacy.[82]

Along with Dan Gillmor of Mediactive, Newmark sat on the advisory board of NewsTrust, an organization that "helps people find and share good journalism online."[83] NewsTrust was the primary instance of news literacy advocacy occurring outside a traditional educational setting, geared towards the American people at large. Up until March 2012, NewsTrust was a "social news network" that aggregated stories from traditional and independent media and used a rating system for readers to review articles using NewsTrust's online tools for better critical discrimination – like TruthSquad, a community fact-checking tool, or MyNews, which sorted stories according to their personal relevance for the reader.

---

[81] Romenesko, Jim. "Craig Newmark: I want to have news again that I can trust." *Romenesko.com,* Nov. 28 2011. http://jimromenesko.com/2011/11/28/craig-newmark-i-want-to-have-news-again-that-i-can-trust/ Accessed 2 Dec 2011.
[82] Newmark, Craig. Craig Connects. 2011. http://www.craigconnects.org Accessed 10 March 2012.
[83] NewsTrust, "About," NewsTrust. 2010. http://newstrust.net/about/press Accessed 4 March 2012.

Fabrice Florin created NewsTrust in 2005 and grew it into a Wikipedia-styled aggregator until funding ran out, despite partnerships with major media outlets and funding from Sunlight, The MacArthur Foundation and Newmark himself. The "experiment," as Florin called it, ceased publishing news in March 2012 and its future is uncertain, potentially finding a new home in another nonprofit.[84] The closure was seen as a major loss in the move for better public journalism. However, NewsTrust also boasted an additional asset – a bevy of news literacy educational materials, including several easily-accessible guides for teachers, students and the general public on the tenets of news literacy and what to look for in quality journalism. These materials promote the mantra "Think like a journalist," in keeping with the Stony Brook and NLP models that make use of journalists themselves to teach news literacy.[85]

Extracurricular news literacy initiatives continue to pop up outside journalistic contexts. Of course, becoming news literate is intricately linked to becoming web-savvy, and so something like Common Sense Media which teaches students to be responsible digital citizens, or something like Scholastic Media's Digital Curriculum & Tools for the 21st Century, include news literacy ideas in their broader lessons. Digital games have become increasingly useful for teaching media literacy to students outside the classroom as even the education reform movement finds more to love about interactive game teaching, but Play the News is the sole

---

[84] Florin, Fabrice. "Next Steps for NewsTrust," *NewsTrust Blog.* Jan. 1, 2012. http://blog.newstrust.net/2012/01/next-steps.html Accessed 2 Feb. 2012.
[85] NewsTrust, Literacy Guides. 2011. http://newstrust.net/guides Accessed 3 March 2012.

example of true news literacy education through game. Play the News, founded in 2008, is where "fantasy sports meets the evening news," engaging players to be more active in news consumption through digital interaction.[86]

Classroom education remains the modus operandi for news literacy programs, though almost always promoted and implemented by a third party not native to the education system (for example, it's rarely the school board itself deciding to incorporate more media and news literacy). And consistently, that external force promoting such education is made of journalists, skewed especially towards newspaper journalists over television or radio; the American Society of Newspaper Editors host a News Literacy Toolkit on its website and offers talking points for convincing educators to jump on the bandwagon, and the Newspaper Association of America Foundation promotes its High Five curriculum merging journalism and language arts.[87] Because of this dominance in education over the Web, games or recreation, my case study reveals the nuances and challenges of a standard news literacy education program and questions opportunities for growth outside secondary education.

---

[86] Play the News, Impact Games. 2008. http://www.playthenewsgame.com. Accessed 1 April 2012.
[87] "News Literacy Toolkit." American Society of Newspaper Editors, 2012. http://asne.org/key_initiatives/youth_journalism/news_literacy_tool_kit.aspx Accessed 4 March 2012.

CHAPTER 5: CASE STUDY FINDINGS

Bethesda – Chevy Chase High School and NLP

Bethesda Chevy-Chase High School is one of four schools in the greater Washington, D.C. area using professional journalists to deliver the NLP curriculum in Honors English and Journalism classes. The high school is located in suburban Washington, D.C., in the affluent area of Montgomery County, Md., and enrolls 1788 students, the majority of whom are Caucasian. B-CC has an International Baccalaureate program as well as Honors and Advanced Placement courses, and 75% of graduates go immediately to a four-year college.[88]

I observed two forty-seven minute classes in one teacher's classroom, one in his Honors English 11 class and one in Journalism 2. The NLP has been incorporated at B-CC High School for the past year, but because students cycle through and graduate, many were experiencing the program for the first time. For the students in the English class especially, the news literacy curriculum was new because most were newly exposed to the production processes of journalism and because the News Literacy Project had just begun there. In the Journalism 2 class, students possessed more advanced news literacy skills due to prior exposure to NLP visits and the nature of their experience in the class producing the school newspaper.

---

[88] "B-CC Profile," *B-CC High School: About Us.* 2011.
http://www.montgomeryschoolsmd.org/uploadedFiles/schools/bcchs/counseling/Newest%20Profile%202010-2011.pdf PDF. Accessed via web 9 March 2012.

Especially relevant to this study is that the school not only has a student-run print newspaper, *The Tattler*, but also publishes an online version, *TattlerExtra*. Both the print and online newspaper are produced in the journalism classes. The online edition of *The Tattler* is significant because it demonstrates a high level of media fluency and Internet dependency among students both producing and consuming the *TattlerExtra*, so much so that the editors, like many professional newsroom editors, found it necessary to publish online:

> We decided to make an online version of *The Tattler* to catch up with modern day technology. Practically all teens today are "tech junkies" and are obsessively communicating with each other through social networking cites such as Facebook, MySpace and Twitter. The online edition will help *The Tattler* keep up with current events. The downside to the print is that the articles are dated, given the nature of it. With the online edition, it can be updated quickly and news stories can be put up the second something happens.[89]

The Wordpress-powered website is impressive for a high school organization, and makes good use of technology including scrolling photo banners, RSS feeds and online forums embedded in the homepage. The paper's content, too, is well written and features advanced reporting and interviewing, such as a front-page interview with Supreme Court justice Elena Kagan. *The Tattler* demonstrates a high level of Web fluency and multimedia dexterity.

Case Study 1: Honors English 11

A NLP visit to an English class is more typical of the program's goals than a visit to a journalism class, since the NLP promotes critical consumption skills as

---

[89] Lazo, Margarita and Lauren Hoover. "About." *The Tattler Extra,* 2009. http://tattlerextra.org/about/

necessary for everyday life, not only for journalists. The February 24 visit featured Henry Schuster, a producer for CBS' *60 Minutes* who was a producer at CNN for 25 years. Schuster's visit coincided with the class unit on nonfiction writing, culminating in each student writing a feature piece on an issue of their choice. Schuster was there to discuss the basics of good reporting and writing for a major feature piece, based on his experiences with *60 Minutes*, and prior to the session the students had already chosen their article topics. They had also prepared a "Feature Story Checklist" with ideas of what goes into a successful feature story piece.

Schuster looked more newsroom-ready than professorial, dressed casually in a red pullover and seated at the head of a large circle of desks, conducive to discussion. The class was racially diverse, with fourteen Caucasians, six African-Americans, one Asian and three Hispanic students, but only five or six female students. It was a Friday morning and the class seemed tired, with many students resting their heads on their desks or sprawling out backwards on their chairs, some even closing their eyes.

Schuster immediately engaged the silent class by asking volunteers to pitch their feature story ideas to him. One or two raised their hands to give a story idea, which Schuster followed up with questions like, "How will you get people to talk about that?" and "Have you thought about interviewing parents?" He then called on others since no more volunteers were forthcoming. Nearly all the pitches were on student life, trending towards the edgy: teen binge drinking culture, how video games affect teen violence, the spread of Adderall abuse, peer pressure concerning sex, high school football rivalries, and unexpected marijuana dealers at B-CC. Schuster did not grapple with the content, but attempted to draw out more excitement from the students about pursuing their chosen topic. For the marijuana dealer story, he asked if the writer had planned on using names, since that might present a problem. "I wasn't planning on using names, I guess," mumbled the student, closing the conversation.

Despite Schuster's high energy levels, real-talk tone and youth-friendly pop culture references, the class largely resisted engagement, speaking only when called upon specifically and not volunteering more than was necessary to answer questions. For the duration of the class, only two students had notebooks out, and only one took notes. When Schuster called upon them, the students were articulate and decently thoughtful – it was Honors English, after all, and they were nearly 18 years old – but rarely went beyond a one-sentence, stilted answer to his questions. There was no thinking out loud, or any evident learning taking place. Schuster relayed some of the standard news literacy principles like verification of sources and the idea of objectivity, and injected his own experience as a feature producer highlighting his four word mantra: "Tell me a story." He wisely tailored his lesson to suit the students' writing focus, and told them, "If you don't care about the story that you're writing, nobody else is…you have to cover not only what, who, where, why and when, but also who cares," an idea that spoke both to this particular class's lack of engagement as well as the importance of believing in the transformative power of journalism. About half the class raised their hands to indicate they had seen an episode of *60 Minutes* before, and Schuster offered some anecdotes from his career that stressed that if the person writing doesn't care about the story, then no reader will, and that "No good story is long enough, and no bad story is short enough," pushing the idea of critical judgment and narrative sense over blind acceptance.

Schuster spent the majority of the class showing and discussing a 12-minute *60 Minutes* piece on PTSD-stricken Iraq war veterans returning to their last battle scene in search of emotional closure. He revealed why he pursued this particular piece, what made it interesting to him and how he answered the "Who Cares" question. He asked the class if they knew anyone personally who had served in Iraq and about three or four students raised their hands, which Schuster used as an example of why news stories like this matter, to spread awareness beyond those directly affected. Further, he spoke about the applicable nature of the story to the students since the Iraq veterans featured were only eighteen and nineteen years old. The class appeared mildly interested in the film as it played and applauded at the conclusion, though some used it as an opportunity to close their eyes.

The post-film discussion was open-ended and centered on the difficulty of interviewing subjects about a sensitive topic and how this might apply to the class's stories on alcohol and drug abuse and other controversial issues. Schuster offered aphoristic advice; when one student pitched a story on a "trend" she witnessed, he carefully guided her to seek more information in official studies: "It may be a trend to you, or it may really be a trend." Schuster, having spent a career learning to read people's faces and connect with sources, was adept at reading the students' moods and knowing how far to push them in his questioning. In this sense, I see the benefit of having a journalist enter the classroom – he can relate to students, it provides a fresh face, and can be marked as a special day for the class. It is unclear, though, if this "special" aspect is positive or negative. Most students appeared to see Schuster's visit as the *absence* of normally scheduled programming, as a guest speaker providing supplementary, non-vital, extracurricular information, freeing them from the responsibility of taking notes or learning the material since it wouldn't be "on the test."

The discussion remained sedate and lackluster for the remainder, except for one moment when Schuster asked a student about her writing process for a story on teenage girls dressing more provocatively and she referenced the current Hollywood film *Project X* in her response. This provoked some enthusiastic commentary and social debate from the class on the merits of the film, much as they would discuss a recent Top 40 single or other pop culture piece. This single bright moment in the class led me to question the effectiveness of news literacy as taught through the tired, strained American education system versus another arena more commonly associated with entertainment or pleasure – for example, pop culture, social media or recreational activity, arenas I will explore in my conclusions.

Schuster's visit was tailored specifically to this one feature-writing project and used the journalistic process as the primary means of conveying news literacy, essentially teaching an understanding of the news business over actual literacy skills, critical thinking or evaluative tools. Areas of news literacy notably absent from this particular lesson were the importance of verified sources, the difference between news and opinion, journalistic bias and the entire online sphere. It was clear that Schuster realized the benefits of news literacy education and the real-world impact that those skills can have, but there was a gap between what he and NLP believed he was teaching and what the students actually latched onto in the classroom setting.

Putting aside the base level of boredom and disengagement evident in this instance, which is perhaps typical of a standard high school classroom, there was still another barrier that Schuster or any guest would have had to overcome to effectively connect with students: the interjection of broad ideas about news literacy into a class with a specific, narrower track of study. Essentially, Schuster was tasked with developing a lesson incorporating the tenets of news literacy that would *also* apply to this class's current unit and project, with insufficient interaction or planning with the teacher beforehand. To attempt to tailor a lesson that will connect with and inspire students with little experience of what these students have already learned or their typical media diet seems ineffective at best and at worst, haphazard.

Case Study 2: Journalism 2

Prior to observing the journalism class, NLP coordinator Maureen Freeman informed me that visits to journalism production classes were not typical of the

NLP's work but that this particular class seemed to get a lot out of the program. This class was Journalism 2, so all students enrolled had participated in producing *The Tattler* for at least one year. The class consisted of 25 students, all Caucasian, equally split between males and females. This was the NLP's third and final guest speaker for this class, and featured Lori Aratani, a staff writer for *The Washington Post*.

Aratani was young, professional and enthusiastic, a dynamic force at the front of the classroom able to hold the class's attention long enough to convey an idea and explain the project. The same restlessness and distraction that challenged Schuster during his visit to Honors English 11 characterized this class as well, though in a slightly more productive manner – the classroom's rowdiness imitated that of a newsroom, the hustle-and-bustle of meetings, editorial conversations and decision-making. Aratani began by congratulating the class on their high-quality newspaper and the seriousness with which they approached it, adding some camp-counselor-esque encouragement: "After having done journalism – meeting deadlines, doing interviews – when it comes to college, you're all gonna rock it," she said. She asked if anyone in the class was thinking about pursuing journalism after high school, and three or four students raised their hands, leading to some halfhearted, slightly jaded commentary from Aratani on the changing industry.

The paper's editor-in-chief was the most engaged member of the class, frequently raising her hand to answer or ask questions and perching, throughout the duration of the class, on a wall above the circle of desks. She seemed excited to have Aratani there, and eager to learn from her, but primarily focused on the paper's publication deadlines and surreptitiously conducted some newspaper business while Aratani spoke. Just like in Schuster's presentation, no students had notebooks out to take notes until prompted by an activity requiring it.

Aratani's method was to walk the students through the process of reporting and writing a challenging story, incorporating news literacy ideas along the way. Many of these students were basically familiar with the production process, so Aratani tried to raise their level of journalistic ethics and practices by presenting more specific circumstances requiring a more critical level of decision-making. She ran through a few PowerPoint slides of news literacy components like "how to know what to believe" and rumor versus fact before proposing a problem for students to solve. Working in groups of six, students were given a situational news tip, an example of a real "murder mystery" story that Aratani had researched and written involving the KBG, a shooting and the International Spy Museum. Aratani told them to take fifteen minutes to parcel out how to best report and write the story in their group. Immediately the "doing" aspect engaged the students, and even though some rolled their eyes at the role-playing task, all participated. The practicality and hands-on nature of this assignment was especially pertinent for a journalism production class, and seemed to involve their critical senses a lot more than a lecture.

After about seven minutes of group work, the students' conversations degraded into social chatter and grew increasingly rambunctious until Freeman, sensing this, stepped up to tell Aratani she could move on to the next part of the lesson since most of the students appeared to have completed the assignment. Since I had witnessed this quick (and temporary) loss of focus among the students, I was relieved to see Freeman step in and assert some direction, revealing the type of administrative control and collaboration between teacher, journalist, and NLP administrator that this program needs, especially at its current grassroots level.

Aratani regrouped the class and after some difficulty getting their attention called upon each group to share their reporting strategy. This included where to get information, how to identify and track down these sources, what to ask in interviews, possible leads to follow if others fall through (like asking for security camera tapes from a building if no witnesses were present) and how to go about writing the story with limited information. The use of group work here was effective, since team reporting is common in journalism, and Aratani related a story to this end. The groups came up with solid responses, though nothing groundbreaking, revealing high levels of critical thinking and problem solving. One group had particularly extensive answers and a plan for reporting and writing, and prompting some discussion on the ways the Internet has changed reporting strategy and how technology can aid information gathering as a reporter, including tracking down camera-phone footage. There was a lot of talk of "these days," as in, "these days, you can look up a phone number on the Web," but the discussion stayed focused on production skills and not on the broader, cultural impact of journalism's changes.

After students presented their proposed plans for reporting, Aratani subtly tested them: "Did anyone have a thesis about how it happened, going in?" I expected this to be a trap, for students to reveal their biases and expectations and for Aratani to nudge them in the direction of a reporter's allegiance to objectivity that it would be best to go in with no particular thesis in mind. Instead, after some students volunteered their ideas of what might have happened in the murder mystery, she agreed and revealed her own thought process reporting this story. She used this, perhaps more effectively, to show that it's okay to have your own biases and expectations, but that you can't publish them unless you verify supporting facts. The class was rapt as she detailed how she pursued the story from beginning to end, how she was able to write the article given the information she had despite having no real conclusion to the case (it was never fully proven), and how she had to keep her personal suspicions out of the final piece due to a lack of evidence. Her storytelling was suspenseful and held the class's interest, until the bell signaling the end of the period interrupted her – and then students hastily grabbed backpacks and exited, cutting off Aratani mid-sentence.

The obvious challenges I witnessed in these classrooms were that of attention and time. The news literacy lessons were conveyed well and made good use of classroom technology to reach students through the media being discussed. The journalists were dynamic figures with a wealth of experience in the field, capable of connecting with students and bestowing knowledge upon them. The students were literate and articulate and familiar with group work. But the limits of available time meant that the lesson was squeezed in to the course's normal run, and because the guest had little planning time with the teacher, seemed abruptly placed into the course's trajectory. Holding the students' attention as a non-teacher challenged both visiting journalists, who were forced to straddle the line between conversational tone (to engage with students) and authoritative (to ensure that progress and learning took place instead of mindless chatter), and the teacher played little role in discipline or co-teaching. The students were polite at best, but far from engaged.

Overall, the journalism class responded far better to the NLP speaker than the English class, but there are a number of factors here: 1) the journalism class has a greater stake in learning news literacy as it is relevant to their assessment in that class, and presumably to their interests, since the course is elective, 2) the journalism class had greater experience with NLP visits and news literacy ideas in general, and 3) the journalism presentation was more hands-on than the English class.

The visible evidence of progress in the journalism class, after three NLP visits, is hopeful for this method; it was clear that many of the tenets of news literacy have taken root among those students, especially in terms of critical decision making and "thinking like a journalist." A more worrying thought is that the journalism classes are, in the end, *not* typical of the NLP's goals and are not the target demographic here, so the progress made is less significant.

Therein lies the limit of news literacy in the classroom. It is beneficial and feasible to improve news literacy rates among journalists, even student journalists, as evident from Aratani's lesson. News literacy initiatives, as I have shown, consistently come from journalists and operate in journalistic realms; it is easy to get the press on board. It is easy to convince those who already value the fourth estate of the need to understand media, and of the need to teach the masses. The challenge is how to get people who do not inherently care about the quality of the news – those who do not have a stake in the news media, emotionally or financially—to not only become more news literate, but to care about their own news literacy and work to improve it.

These two NLP visits were overall successful if they are to be judged as a supplemental guest speaker program, but any impact beyond that is difficult to gauge given the seemingly disengaged students. The classroom model of the NLP is far from perfect, but because it is so young, it is reasonable to expect that this system will change to better suit the needs of those involved. I will outline a number of ideas for reform in my conclusions, focusing on better preparation between the teacher and the visiting journalist, the inclusion of post-lesson follow-up through pamphlets or online resources, and increased workshop time over lecture or discussion. Beyond the reform possible within this model, however, there are still some standout issues that deserve to be examined more closely.

Having spent time in youth journalism conferences, I can attest that these programs – which typically bring career journalists to interested students in a similar lecture-and-questions style – are effective, like any course, if your heart is already in the subject matter, or if the speaker is able to convince you quickly that you ought to care. The mixture of philosophical aphorisms and practical advice can be inspiring and can make a real difference in a young journalist's work and career, but are meaningless if there's nothing at stake, as may be the case for a typical, non-journalism student.

That's not to say that passion is necessary to learn – algebra is institutionalized in American schooling, and most learn that without a true passion for the subject, just like grammar and chemistry concepts. But news literacy is a subject that is not tested in the classroom – it's tested every day, on the Internet, in social media and among peers. It is a life skill. The consequences of being news illiterate are very real, but very subtle in the short-term, and will never make themselves manifest through a bad grade or an erroneous re-tweet. Rather, they will become evident later down the line en masse, as consumers determine the axes upon which we judge news. A news literate public will insist on holding news sources accountable and delivering judgment according to reliability and quality. A news illiterate public will place less value upon truth, accuracy and fact-checking, thereby flooding the digital sphere with "junk" and failing to distinguish valuable information, thereby perpetuating the problem.

CHAPTER 6: CONCLUSIONS

Immediate findings

My experience at B-CC High School cast a tone of concern for the future of news literacy programs in secondary education. The News Literacy Project essentially takes the role of a "guest lecture" series, which marks journalists' visits as extracurricular (in tone and student perception) even though they occur within the classroom setting. The result is a program that edges towards Career Day more than actual news literacy skill-building. While the program coordinators, the journalists and the teachers are well-versed in the goals of news literacy education, these concepts are not conveyed with sufficient urgency to the students. That gap in understanding is the primary source of the evident ineffectiveness. Of course, many of my immediate concerns may be mitigated by the fact that such a program could improve over time, and certainly could thrive with more funding and national attention, but at *this* time it is clear that the grassroots approach to news literacy is not sufficient for creating a more news literate public. Thus, while I have suggestions for improvement within the program and for expansion of the program, I will also propose movement towards a more radical solution – teaching news literacy outside the education system.

At B-CC High School I witnessed bored students disengaged with the news literacy presentations despite the variety of multimedia tactics and hands-on activities used. This made clear the massive challenges to implementing any sort of news literacy training in an already strained and arguably "broken" education system. American public schools today face immense obstacles to student success, and it is no secret that more and more education reform groups choose to work outside of the traditional education system to improve students' options through charter schools, online learning, homeschooling and private schools. If even secondary education reformers are seeking new venues for reform, alternative to within the education system itself, news literacy advocates might be wise to follow suit. It is not only difficult to overcome the practical barriers of bureaucracy and tradition in schools, but potentially fruitless: because many students consider school to be an inconvenient, dreary task, an unappealing but necessary evil, including news literacy in the school environment could dampen student interest in the subject.

Further, why insist on fitting news literacy lessons into compulsory education when another sphere offers more possibilities for creative teaching, student engagement and self-motivation? The Internet is a globalized, modern-day salon, where real change and progress flourish. It is, in many ways, the antithesis of the traditional school classroom, with lines blurred between "teacher" and "student" and content linked together not in predetermined units, but through metadata that more closely resembles brain synapses. Even more significantly, the Internet is where students already are, in massive numbers, logging hours and hours of Web time every day, in exactly the venue that demands updated media and news literacy skills. Opportunities abound for embedding news literacy education in social media and the recreational parts of the Internet, and I will address these below.

As for the News Literacy Project and the Center for News Literacy, these programs are clearly doing good work and should be commended for early detection of the need for news literacy education. Both institutions have had a remarkable scope and impact so far, given the grassroots nature of the movement. I would like to see these classroom-based programs expand to far greater scales and push news literacy to a national dialogue so that it is included in every student's curriculum, not as a guest-lecture or a brief unit, but as a consistent, core underpinning of American education. There are infinite ways for teachers to invoke news literacy without a specified unit; by requiring students to defend their sources for assignments, for example, or by identifying "Information Neighborhoods" for each reading. News literacy concepts should be so entrenched in and applicable to the rest of the curriculum (because they are, essentially, critical reading, thinking and skepticism) that students understand them inherently. For an American history class, teachers might mention the role of the press during the civil rights movement, or the rise of radio in the 1930s to disseminate weather information to farmers. In government or international history, a debate on press freedoms could illustrate the ramifications of different government or economic models. In economics, social studies, or even math, students could discuss the use of advertising in cable television news, product placement and false reports, and demographic statistics or data mining. News literacy does not have to be taught explicitly and independently if it is incorporated implicitly throughout the entire curriculum. In addition, it should be made clear to the students that gaining these skills is of utmost importance, as the benefits will not only be immediately evident in students' daily Internet use but will also serve students long after high school graduation. Increased use of "real life" examples in classroom lessons will help students understand that news literacy can be learned in the classroom but is ultimately used in both academic and recreational information gathering.

Still, since these two classroom-based programs are the largest existing methods for news literacy education, and will likely gain momentum in the next few years, it is worth maintaining and expanding their operations at this time while a better method is concurrently developed. Some news literacy education is certainly better than none, and both the Center for News Literacy and the News Literacy Project are making significant progress on this very important issue.

Suggestions for Improvement of Existing Models

While Powers, in his dissertation, offered many ways to overcome barriers that might prevent news literacy implementation in schools and declared that news literacy programs should expand to the national level, I will make several suggestions that these specific programs should adopt before expansion. Nevertheless, my ultimate suggestion for news literacy education through secondary schooling, which must be taken with a grain of salt given the very real funding and bureaucratic barriers to swift change, is in line with Powers' claim: that news literacy instruction must move past the grassroots level of operation as soon as possible. Such a sweeping proposal presents practical obstacles, not ideological ones, but I find that the one-teacher-at-a-time method prevents news literacy concepts from taking root in students' minds because it construes news literacy as non-essential, supplementary education. Operationally, I would like to see the NLP and the Center for News Literacy lobby entire states to make news literacy a required part of teacher training and student curriculum, with a national campaign to raise awareness of the importance of digital, media and news literacy. I would like to see the Department of Education recognize news literacy as an area of focus, hear politicians mention it in campaign platforms, and move discussions on the subject to a national discourse. Through increased collaborations with media literacy advocacy groups and the private sector IT community, as well as the mainstream media, news literacy will gain greater awareness and traction. For example, *GOOD* magazine recently ran a feature on easy tasks to perform to be a better citizen; "Citizenship Task 2" was to read two opposing articles on the same topic, an assignment that is drawn from the news literacy philosophy.[90] More instances of the press or the private sector promoting engaged citizenship (like *GOOD*) boosts the foundation for demanding better news literacy education.

On the ground, here are some immediate changes that would improve the current model:

1. **Broader dissemination of open-source classroom materials and teacher training.** Stony Brook and the NLP maintain a tight control on the curriculum and materials for news literacy instruction. Perhaps

---

[90] "GOOD Citizenship Task 2, Thirty Days of Good." *GOOD*, Feb. 3 2012. http://www.good.is/post/good-citizenship-task-2-read-two-opposing-opinion-pieces-on-the-same-topic-30daysofgood/ **Accessed 4 March 2012.**

this is for financial reasons – not wanting to give away well-developed material for free – but also, perhaps, so that only approved, properly instructed teachers can access the material and teach news literacy. This makes little sense, since the NLP requires no training of its journalist lecturers, who are even less equipped than the classroom teachers for this role. It is easy to understand the motivation behind wanting to ensure that the right message is taught, but such an attempt at total oversight handicaps the movement's growth. By making open-source lesson plans and curriculum ideas available online to all teachers, not just those approved by the NLP and Stony Brook, news literacy can spread more freely to more classrooms.

2. **Increased communication and collaboration between teachers and visiting journalists**. Stony Brook's teacher-training model is effective in that it gives teachers the tools to encourage news literacy year-round. The NLP model benefits from the career authority that a journalist brings, but suffers from an intermittent visit schedule. By merging these organizations' two strengths and requiring journalists and teachers to prepare for the unit more comprehensively, students will gain a more thorough education. More importantly, the impression that their teachers and professional journalists are teaming up to drive home the importance of news literacy will help establish the perception that this is a truly urgent and essential part of secondary education.

3. **Earlier intervention.** Stony Brook addresses news literacy largely among college students and the NLP targets grades six through twelve, but a greater emphasis needs to be placed on middle school and possibly elementary school students as students begin using digital media at earlier ages. Children are constantly surrounded by news and information via television, advertising, radio and the Internet, and embedding news literacy tenets in elementary and middle school critical reading curriculum helps set the tone that news literacy is a skill for *life*.

4. **Insistence on immediate, extracurricular "real-life" application of lessons.** In the same way that health classes develop lifelong habits rather than teach material for a specific one-time assessment, news literacy should be presented to students as a healthy mental habit necessary for participating in the modern media landscape, and, more broadly, modern society. Once students see how increased news literacy affects their everyday media usage, they will be more likely to engage with the news literacy curriculum and internalize its lessons.

Proposals for Moving Beyond the Classroom

As stated earlier, while existing education programs are beneficial overall and with a few reforms could reach even greater levels of effectiveness, given my findings, I insist on serious consideration of teaching news literacy outside the classroom. In an ideal world, news literacy would be both taught in the classroom *and* embedded in social media and the Internet to create a pervasive message and a revaluation of quality news for all Americans. But until that becomes possible, there is no reason why the tenets of news literacy cannot be incorporated into the spheres that use them most – online news, social media and blogs. Below, a few specific ways in which this can be accomplished:

1. **The power of pop culture.** The one moment of excitement in the classes I witnessed came when a student referenced the Hollywood film *Project X*, then in theaters. To students, that was worth talking about – they could relate, share opinions and connect over the movie. News literacy curriculum can harness this captivating power of pop culture by demonstrating that news literacy concepts apply to what students enjoy most. Entertainment, like news, is consumed largely on the Web. If students would rather read articles or watch YouTube clips about movies, music and celebrities than foreign policy or local headlines, lessons should focus on the literacy objective rather than the subject. Method trumps content here. In addition, news literacy advocates should promote critical thinking and digital savvy as something "popular" in itself, making it "cool" to think before re-tweeting and socially frowned-upon to read online articles without checking sources first.

2. **Interactive games.** Online games have become increasingly appealing for teaching concepts in the last decade, from math to spelling to the realities of poverty.[91] In the news sphere, there are a number of "current event" games testing news knowledge, "community games" that highlight major issues and reveal surprising truths for the game user, and "Play the News," mentioned earlier as a game that allows players to follow a news story through publication.[92] Journalist-player games like "Global Conflicts: Palestine" can show users what it is like to report a story, and literacy games improve reading and writing skills. Admongo, a game developed by the Federal Trade Commission, educates kids ages 8-12 on how to discern commercial advertising from news, and the Knight Foundation awarded a News Challenge grant to Georgia Tech's "Newsgames" project to look more closely at using interactive games to teach journalism. This field is growing; combining recreation, news literacy and the "achievement" mentality, online games present a wide-open, largely untapped opportunity for news literacy to reach more students more effectively. In Sissel McCarthy's course, the most effective lesson was the one in which her undergraduates developed interactive classroom games and

---

[91] There are a number of examples, but most recently "Spent," (http://playspent.org/) developed by Urban Ministries of Durham in North Carolina, walks users through a month living in poverty to increase empathy; similarly, "Third World Farmer" (http://www.3rdworldfarmer.com) sheds light on the world's economic disparities.
[92] Schweizer, Bobby. "A History of Newsgames." PBS Interactive. Dec. 14, 2010. http://www.pbs.org/idealab/2010/12/a-brief-history-of-newsgames-combining-news-videogames341.html Accessed 1 April 2012.

played them with students (offline, in person).[93] This success can be translated to the online sphere for maximum effect with minimal tax on human resources.

3. **Better "truth goggles" on websites.** This task falls on the part of news producers and Web developers more than consumers, but consumers play a key role in the equation. "Truth goggles" might consist of a small box on a webpage, in a browser plug-in or in the corner of a television screen that ranks the article's reliability, voted on by viewers. Clicking would expand the box to show more information on sources, fact-checking background and questionable claims. Low reliability rankings could translate to lower-ranked Google search results. NewsTrust attempted this with some success before they ceased operations, but if such an idea was mandatory for all television and Internet news it would *massively* shift the media landscape from one focused on clicks, page views and search engine optimized headlines, to one operating along the axes of reliable and unreliable news. In other words: it could lead to a drastically improved information ecosystem, precisely what the future of the Internet – and the future of the news media – needs.

4. **Credentials for reliability.** Taking the "truth goggles" idea further, news sources with consistently high reliability ratings could be marked

---

[93] McCarthy, Sissel

with a credential so that individual articles do not require time-consuming assessment. This credential would apply cross-platform to television, radio, online and print news, and would be prominently displayed on news pages (or read aloud, on radio). Over time, such a credential – similar to those administered by the American National Standards Institute – would become highly sought after for any news organization attempting to seriously publish well-reported, fact-checked news. Meanwhile, individual citizen blogs and advertisements disguised as news could be allowed to flourish in the name of free speech, but consumers would have sufficient resources to guide news consumption decisions.

5. **Social Media Responsibility.** Because news spreads fastest through Twitter and Facebook – and in the future, presumably, other yet-unknown social media outlets—these should be included in the framework for teaching news literacy on the Internet. Here it would be most prudent to combine media and news literacy, perhaps in an online "What to Know Before Using Facebook" primer course required for all new registered users. The course could cover privacy issues and implications of posting unverified information, and could direct users to more news literacy resources Further, every time social media users engage with news via social media (either by Facebook liking, re-

posting or re-tweeting) users could be asked to rank the reliability of the news source, in keeping with the "Truth Goggles" idea posed above.

Disruption and Opportunity: America at a Crossroads

Ultimately, all of my proposals for increasing news literacy outside traditional education structures rely on harnessing the power of the Internet. The Internet has driven innovation in many spheres – commerce, entertainment, politics, government, recreation, shopping – and if news literacy advocates can collaborate with technology leaders and educators to work with the possibilities of the Web, news literacy has a far brighter future in America.

The Pew Research Center's Internet and American Life project recently released "The Future of the Internet 2012," a landmark report that makes it all too clear how massively the Internet will inform and shape American society in the next decade. Assessing a broad swath of technology stakeholders and critics, the report determined the "most desired life skills" for young people in 2020 to include:

1. The ability to search effectively for information online and to be able to discern the quality and veracity of the information one finds and communicate these findings well (referred to as digital literacy)
2. Synthesizing (being able to bring together details from across many sources)
3. The ability to distinguish between the "noise" and the message in the ever-growing sea of information[94]

---

[94] Pew Internet and American Life Project, "The Future of the Internet." Pew Research Center, 2012. http://pewInternet.org/~/media//Files/Reports/2012/PIP_Future_of_Internet_2012_Young_brains_PDF.pdf Accessed 1 April 2012.

These are all in sync with the goals of the news literacy movement and further demonstrate the urgency for national attention at this juncture. The findings of the report are most emotively summed up by Barry Chudakov, a research fellow at the McLuhan Program in Culture and Technology at the University of Toronto:

> "[By 2020] technology will be so seamlessly integrated into our lives that it will effectively disappear. The line between self and technology is thin today; by then it will effectively vanish. We will think with, think into, and think through our smart tools but their presence and reach into our lives will be less visible. The cognitive challenge children and youth will face is integrity…There will be a premium on the skill of maintaining presence, of mindfulness, of awareness in the face of persistent and pervasive tool extensions and incursions into our lives. Is this my intention, or is the tool inciting me to feel and think this way? That question, more than multitasking or brain atrophy due to accessing collective intelligence via the Internet, will be the challenge of the future."[95]

I find it fortuitous that such a forward-thinking assessment, like this report, is happening at the same time that news literacy efforts are expanding and newsrooms are increasingly collaborating with technology innovators. This marks our age as one of significant disruption, in which the very structures that defined America for so long – the authority of the press, the rigid, compulsory nature of the education system, and the binary producer/consumer model – are reshuffled and replaced by a new reigning hierarchy of American values, like the power of the individual, participatory education and news consumption, and free, unfettered access to a broad variety of information. Such creative destruction is part of the natural cycle of history, and is key to reinventing and improving any society. As

---

[95] Pew Internet and American Life Project, "The Future of the Internet."

became evident in the transformation of the press and the Web in the last decade, America now finds herself on the verge of a new societal, political and cultural order, driven by changes both incremental and revolutionary that will define our common culture for many years until the next great shift.

We can move seamlessly and with great enthusiasm into the new technological age only if consumers are sufficiently prepared with the tools and knowledge necessary to determine a positive future for American media. News literacy is at the core of this argument, and I have no doubt the need for increased news literacy will only prove to be more pertinent over the next decade. To that end, we must aggressively pursue the best possible education method for edifying news literacy skills in the American public, which requires further trial-and-error and constant critical self-analysis. The existing efforts are to be commended for early action and noble pursuit of improved education, but we have a long way to go to move news literacy to the national consciousness it deserves, and further still to implement this curriculum effectively and comprehensively. Once this occurs, American society will vastly benefit tremendously from a more engaged, informed citizenry, a liberated and thriving press, and a true democracy worthy of the high ideals upon which it was founded.

Bibliography

"B-CC Profile," *B-CC High School: About Us.* 2011. http://www.montgomeryschoolsmd.org/uploadedfiles. PDF, Accessed via web 9 March 2012.

"GOOD Citizenship Task 2, Thirty Days of Good." *GOOD*, Feb. 3 2012. http://www.good.is/post/good-citizenship-task-2-read-two-opposing-opinion-pieces-on-the-same-topic-30daysofgood/ Accessed 4 March 2012.

"J-Lab: Staff," "About." J Lab, 2011. http://www.j-lab.org/about/staff. Accessed 10 Dec. 2011.

"Media Education Lab Convening October 23-25, 2008," *Youth Media Reporter* blog. 19 Sept 2008. http://www.youthmediareporter.org/2008/09/media_education_lab_convening.html. Accessed 6 March 2012.

"News Literacy Toolkit." American Society of Newspaper Editors, 2012. http://asne.org/key_initiatives/youth_journalism/news_literacy_tool_kit.aspx Accessed 4 March 2012.

"Newspapers in Education: History." *Newspapers in Education*, 2010. http://www.nieworld.com/niehistory.htm. Accessed 9 March 2012.

"The Nation's Report Card." The National Assessment Governing Board, a branch of the U.S. Department of Education. June-August 2011. Reports available at www.nationsreportcard.gov.

"*The New York Times* joins Mozilla and Knight Foundation to Drive Open Innovation in News," *Mozilla* blog, March 9 2012. http://blog.mozilla.com/blog/2012/03/09/new-york-times-joins-mozilla/ Accessed 15 March 2012.

"The News Literacy Project Kicks Off DC Expansion with an Event Featuring Gwen Ifill: Press Release." *E.L. Haynes Newsletter*. August 28, 2011. http://www.elhaynes.org/news.html Accessed 13 Jan 2012.

"Third World Farmer." 3rd World Farmer Team, 2012. www.3rdworldfarmer.com. Accessed 9 March 2012.

Aufderheide, Patricia. "Media Literacy: A Report of the National Leadership Conference on Media Literacy," Aspen Institute, Communications and Society Program, 1993. http://eric.ed.gov/ Accessed 20 Oct. 2011.

Barnhurst, Kevin and John Nerone. *The Form of News: A History*. New York: The Guilford Press, 2001.

Bowman, Shayne and Willis, Chris. "We Media: How Audiences Are Shaping the Future of News and Information," The Media Center at The American Press Institute, Sept. 21 2003. http://www.hypergene.net/wemedia/weblog.php Accessed 22 Oct. 2011.

Center for News Literacy, "Who? What? Why? Where? When? The Conference at a Glance," March 2011. http://newsliteracyconference.com/content/?page_id=1102 Accessed 13 Jan 2012.

Clarke, Adele. *Situational Analysis: Grounded Theory After the Postmodern Turn*. Thousand Oaks, CA: Sage, 2005. Cited in Hammersly and Atkinson, *Ethnography: Principles in Practice*, 167.

Coll, Steve. "Think Tank: It's About the Journalism," *The New Yorker*, March 16 2009. http://www.newyorker.com/online/blogs/stevecoll/2009/03/its-about-the-j.html Accessed 10 December 2011.

Coll, Steve. "Think Tank: The Future of Journalism," *The New Yorker*, May 7 2009. http://www.newyorker.com/online/blogs/stevecoll/2009/05/the-future-of-journalism.html Accessed 10 Dec. 2011.

Common Core State Standards Initiative, 2011. www.corestandards.org.

Digital Classroom, The Newseum. 2011. http://www.newseum.org/digitalclassroom/video/news-apps/default.aspx Accessed 3 March 2012.

E.L. Haynes Charter School, "About." 2011. http://www.elhaynes.org/aboutus.html Accessed 9 March 2012.

Eaves, David. "Not Brain Candy: A Review of *The Information Diet* by Clay Johnson." *Eaves.ca*, Dec. 15, 2011. http://eaves.ca/2011/12/15/not-brain-candy-a-review-of-the-information-diet-by-clay-johnson/ Accessed 13 January 2012.

Edelman, "2012 Trust Barometer Infographic," *Edelman Insights 2012*. http://www.slideshare.net/EdelmanInsights/trust-bar-fin. Accessed 1 March 2012.

Fancher, Michael R. *Of the Press: Models for Transforming American*

Journalism, A Report of the Aspen Institute Forum on Communication and Society. Washington, DC: Aspen Institute, Communications and Society Program, 2010. Print.

Florin, Fabrice. "Next Steps for NewsTrust," *NewsTrust Blog.* Jan. 1, 2012. http://blog.newstrust.net/2012/01/next-steps.html Accessed 3 March 2012.

Ford, Eliza. Phone interview by Caroline Klibanoff. Digital audio recording, March 8 2012, Washington D.C.

Glaser, Barney G & Strauss, Anselm L. *The Discovery of Grounded Theory: Strategies for Qualitative Research.* Chicago: Aldine Publishing Company, 1967. Print.

Hacks/Hackers "About." *Hacks/Hackers* blog, 2010. http://hackshackers.com/about/ Accessed 13 Jan 2012.

Hammersly, Martyn and Atkinson, Paul. *Ethnography: Principles in Practice*, third edition. Routledge: London, 1983, 2007. Print.

Hobbs, Renee. "Digital and Media Literacy: A Plan of Action," A White Paper. The Aspen Institute Communications and Society Program, 2010. PDF.

Hobbs, Renee. "News Literacy: What Not to Do," *Nieman Reports Summer 2011 Online Exclusives.* Summer 2011. http://www.nieman.harvard.edu/reportsitem.aspx?id=102645 Accessed 10 Dec 2011.

Inside the Guardian Blog, "Lessons from our Open News Trial," *The Guardian UK.* Oct. 17, 2011. http://www.guardian.co.uk/help/insideguardian/2011/oct/17/guardian-newslist Accessed 12 March 2012.

Jarvis, Jeff. *Public Parts: How Sharing in the Digital Age Improves the Way We Work and Live.* New York: Simon & Shuster, 2011. Print.

Johnson, Clay. *The Information Diet.* California: O'Reilly Media Inc., 2012. Print.

Knight Commission on the Information Needs of Communities, *Informing Communities: Sustaining Democracy in the Digital Age.* The Aspen Institute: Washington, D.C. 2009. http://www.knightcomm.org Accessed 10 Dec 2011.

Lazo, Margarita and Lauren Hoover. "About." *The Tattler Extra,* 2009. http://tattlerextra.org/about/ Accessed 9 March 2012.

Loth, Renee. "Teaching News Literacy in the Digital Age," *The Chronicle Review*. Feb. 5, 2012. http://chronicle.com/article/Teaching-News-Literacy-in-the/130613/?sid=cr&utm_source=cr&utm_medium=en Accessed 13 Jan 2012.

Matlack, Tom, "The Rebirth of Newspapers," *The Huffington Post*. May 18, 2011. http://www.huffingtonpost.com/tom-matlack/ny-times-paywall-_b_863745.html Accessed 12 Nov 2011.

McCarthy, Sissel. Interview by Caroline Klibanoff. MP3 Audio Recording, Caribou Coffee, Atlanta, Georgia. Jan. 8, 2012.

McChesney, Robert and Victor Pickard, ed. *Will the Last Reporter Please Turn Out the Lights? The Collapse of Journalism and What Can Be Done to Fix It*. New York: The New Press, 2011. Print.

McClelland, Mac. "What is Good Fact-Checking?" *Mother Jones*, Dec. 21 2011. http://motherjones.com/media/2011/12/mac-mcclelland-burma-fact-checking-politifact Accessed 13 Jan 2012.

Miller, Dean. "Want Better Journalism? Boost News Literacy," *The Christian Science Monitor*. Stony Brook, NY, Jan. 14 2010. Print.

Newmark, Craig. Craig Connects. 2011. http://www.craigconnects.org Accessed 10 March 2012.

NewsTrust, Literacy Guides. 2011. http://newstrust.net/guides Accessed 3 March 2012.

NewsTrust, "About," NewsTrust. 2010. http://newstrust.net/about/press Accessed 4 March 2012.

Obama, Barack. "Remarks by the President at University of Michigan Spring Commencement." Michigan Stadium, Ann Arbor, MI. 1 May 2010. Keynote address. Cited by Powers, 10.

Paton, John, "WAN IFRA International Newsroom Summit: How the Crowd Saved Our Company," *Digital First,* Jun 8 2011. http://jxpaton.wordpress.com/2011/06/08/wan_ifra/ Accessed 10 Dec. 2011.

Paulson, Ken. Interview by Caroline Klibanoff. Digital film recording. The Newseum, Washington, D.C., Dec. 6 2011.

Pew Internet and American Life Project, "Internet Overtakes Newspapers as News

Source," Pew Research Center, 2008. http://pewresearch.org/pubs/1066/Internet-overtakes-newspapers-as-news-source Accessed 2 Nov 2011.

Pew Internet and American Life Project, "The Future of the Internet." Pew Research Center, 2012. http://pewInternet.org/~/media//Files/Reports/2012/PIP_Future_of_Internet_2012_Young_brains_PDF.pdf Accessed 1 April 2012.

Powers, Elia, "Teaching News Literacy in the Age of New Media: Why Secondary School Students Should be Taught to Judge the Credibility of the News they Consume," Master's Dissertation, Washington University in St. Louis, August 2010. PDF.

Play the News, Impact Games. 2008. http://www.playthenewsgame.com. Accessed 1 April 2012.

Purcell, Kristen et al, "Understanding the Participatory News Consumer," The Internet and American Life Project, Pew Research Center. March 1, 2010. PDF via http://www.pewInternet.org. Accessed 10 Dec. 2011.

Register Citizen. "What the Newsroom Café taught us about improving local journalism," *Register Citizen Open Newsroom Project blog.* Sep. 13, 2011 http://newsroomcafe.wordpress.com/ Accessed 13 Jan 2012.

Romenesko, Jim. "Craig Newmark: I want to have news again that I can trust." *Romenesko.com,* Nov. 28 2011. http://jimromenesko.com/2011/11/28/craig-newmark-i-want-to-have-news-again-that-i-can-trust/ Accessed 3 Dec 2011.

Rosen, Jay. "The Psychology of Bloggers vs. Journalists: My Talk at South by Southwest." *PressThink.org,* March 12, 2011. http://pressthink.org/2011/03/the-psychology-of-bloggers-vs-journalists-my-talk-at-south-by-southwest/ Accessed 10 Dec. 2011.

Salvador, Michael and Sias, Patricia ed. The *Public Voice in a Democracy at Risk.* Westport, CT: Praeger, 1998. Accessed via Google Books, 20 Nov. 2011.

Schweizer, Bobby. "A History of Newsgames." PBS Interactive. Dec. 14, 2010. http://www.pbs.org/idealab/2010/12/a-brief-history-of-newsgames-combining-news-videogames341.html Accessed 1 April 2012.

Shafer, Jack. "Media bias? Give me more, please!" *Reuters,* Sept. 20 2011. http://blogs.reuters.com/jackshafer/2011/09/20/media-bias-give-me-more-please/ Accessed 10 Dec. 2011.

Shafer, Jack. "Why Media Bias Isn't a Journalistic Problem," open interview moderated by Mallary Jean Tenore. Online Chat, Poynter.org, Sep. 21 2011 http://www.poynter.org/latest-news/top-stories/146685/live-chat-today-with-jack-shafer-why-media-bias-isnt-a-journalistic-problem/

Shirky, Clay. "Are Newspapers Finally Figuring Out How to Reward Their Best Customers?" *Paid Content*, Jan. 4 2012. http://paidcontent.org/article/419-are-newspapers-finally-figuring-out-how-to-reward-their-best-customers/P1/ Accessed online Jan. 4 2012.

Shirky, Clay. "Why We Need the News Environment to Be Chaotic," *Clay Shirky*, July 9 2011. http://www.shirky.com/weblog/2011/07/we-need-the-new-news-environment-to-be-chaotic/ Accessed 10 Dec. 2011

Smith, Erica. "Paper Cuts." 2012. www.newspaperlayoffs.com Accessed 3 March 2012.

Starkman, Dean. "Confidence Game: The Limited Vision of the News Gurus," *Columbia Journalism Review*, Nov/Dec 2011. http://www.cjr.org/essay/confidence_game.php Accessed 10 Dec 2011

Swensen, David and Schmidt, Michael, "News You Can Endow." *The New York Times* (Op-Ed), January 27, 2009. http://www.nytimes.com/2009/01/28/opinion/28swensen.html Accessed 10 Dec. 2011.

The Center for News Literacy, "Emory University Launches News Literacy Course," *News*. March 2, 2012. http://www.centerfornewsliteracy.org/?p=1178 Accessed 13 Jan 2012.

The Center for News Literacy, "The Stony Brook Model." 2011. http://www.centerfornewsliteracy.org/?p=47 Accessed 13 Jan 2012.

The News Literacy Project. "About," "Program." *The News Literacy Project*. 2011. http://www.thenewsliteracyproject.org/about/ Accessed 13 Jan 2012.

The News Literacy Project. "Banner Year in 2011," *The News Literacy Project Blog*. Dec.2011.http://www.thenewsliteracyproject.org/blog/the_news_literacy_project_concludes_a_banner_year_in_2011/ Accessed 13 Jan 2012.

The News Literacy Project, "PBS NewsHour Reports on the News Literacy Project,"

The News Literacy Project Blog. Dec. 2011. http://www.thenewsliteracyproject.org/blog/pbs_newshour_reports_on_the_news_literacy_project/ Accessed 13 Jan 2012.

The Sunlight Foundation, "About," "Sunlight Labs," "Sunlight Reporting." 2011. www.sunlightfoundatoin.com Accessed 3 March 2012.

Urban Ministries of Durham, "Spent." 2012. www.playspent.org. Accessed 9 March 2012.

Waldman, Steven and the Working Group on Information Needs of Communities. *The Information Needs of Communities: The Changing Media Landscape in a Broadband Age.* Federal Communications Commission, July 2011. www.fcc.gov/infoneedsreport.

Wolchover, Natalie. "People Aren't Smart Enough for Democracy to Flourish, Scientists Say." Yahoo! News, Feb. 28 2012. http://news.yahoo.com/people-arent-smart-enough-democracy-flourish-scientists-185601411.html Accessed 9 March 2012.